Joyce,

Be filled continually and with the Holy Spirit and your hearts will overflow with a joyful song to the Lord. Encourage each others with words of scripture, singing the Psalms with praises and spontaneous songs given by the Spirit.

~ Ephesians 5:18b-19 TPT

Sing to the Lord a New Song

Menika ♡
2024

CALLED TO SING

A THEOLOGICAL OVERVIEW & PRACTICAL GUIDE TO PROPHETIC SINGING

RACHEL CULVER

FOREWORD BY
LEE M. CUMMINGS

WESTBOW
PRESS®
A DIVISION OF THOMAS NELSON
& ZONDERVAN

Copyright © 2021 Rachel Culver.

All rights reserved. No part of this book may be used or reproduced by any means, graphic, electronic, or mechanical, including photocopying, recording, taping or by any information storage retrieval system without the written permission of the author except in the case of brief quotations embodied in critical articles and reviews.

This book is a work of non-fiction. Unless otherwise noted, the author and the publisher make no explicit guarantees as to the accuracy of the information contained in this book and in some cases, names of people and places have been altered to protect their privacy.

WestBow Press books may be ordered through booksellers or by contacting:

WestBow Press
A Division of Thomas Nelson & Zondervan
1663 Liberty Drive
Bloomington, IN 47403
www.westbowpress.com
844-714-3454

Because of the dynamic nature of the Internet, any web addresses or links contained in this book may have changed since publication and may no longer be valid. The views expressed in this work are solely those of the author and do not necessarily reflect the views of the publisher, and the publisher hereby disclaims any responsibility for them.

Any people depicted in stock imagery provided by Getty Images are models, and such images are being used for illustrative purposes only. Certain stock imagery © Getty Images.

Scripture quotations taken from The Holy Bible, New International Version® NIV® Copyright © 1973 1978 1984 2011 by Biblica, Inc. TM. Used by permission. All rights reserved worldwide.

Scripture quotations taken from the Amplified® Bible (AMPC), Copyright © 1954, 1958, 1962, 1964, 1965, 1987 by The Lockman Foundation Used by permission. www.Lockman.org

Scripture quotations are from the ESV® Bible (The Holy Bible, English Standard Version®), copyright © 2001 by Crossway, a publishing ministry of Good News Publishers. Used by permission. All rights reserved.

Scripture taken from the King James Version of the Bible.

Scripture quotations taken from the (NASB®) New American Standard Bible®, Copyright © 1960, 1971, 1977, 1995, 2020 by The Lockman Foundation. Used by permission. All rights reserved. www.lockman.org

Scripture taken from the New King James Version® Copyright © 1982 by Thomas Nelson. Used by permission. All rights reserved.

Emphasis in bold typeface of Scripture was added by the author.

ISBN: 978-1-6642-4890-8 (sc)
ISBN: 978-1-6642-4891-5 (hc)
ISBN: 978-1-6642-4889-2 (e)

Library of Congress Control Number: 2021922209

Printed in he United States of America.

WestBow Press rev. date: 12/18/2021

I encourage all singers and worship leaders to read this amazing book, *Called to Sing*. It is a bold and clear message on an underwritten but vital topic—prophetic singing. Rachel does an incredible job of providing a theological framework and a wealth of practical instruction from someone who has been singing prophetically for decades. Rachel was a faithful worship leader and prophetic singer at IHOP–KC for many years. She continues to sing prophetically in the house of prayer in Kalamazoo and to train and shepherd young singers and worship leaders. She has depth of insight because of her depth of experience in singing the songs of His heart. I highly recommend this!

—Mike Bickle, International House of Prayer of Kansas City

Rachel takes a "machete to the jungle" for us and paves a clear and easy to understand path for what it means to be a prophetic singer. Many will reap the rewards of her years of experience and hard work!

—Katie Reed, Worship Director at Radiant Church in Kansas City

In heartfelt, conversational style, Rachel Culver shows how the songs of salvation are accessible to all. You're about to be inspired to release the praises of Jesus like never before!

—Bob Sorge, Author of *Exploring Worship* and *Next Wave*

The Bible is very clear that before the Lord returns, He is going to awaken prophetic songs across the earth. Isaiah saw these days coming when he declared, "From the ends of the earth we've heard songs, 'Glory to the Righteous One!'" Songs to Jesus and about Jesus are going to fill the earth, and it will be these songs that will beckon Him to return. God has been awakening His people to this reality over the last twenty years, and He has raised up mothers and fathers to train a generation in it. Rachel Culver is one of these mothers who has invested thousands of hours over the last twenty years to the glory, dignity, and profound power of prophetic singing. In this book, *Called to Sing*, she takes the wealth of revelation of what she has received from God in prophetic singing and lays out a roadmap for all of us. I'm convinced we are going to see a whole new generation of prophetic singers arise because they read this book and it awakened something so deep in them. My prayer is that hundreds of thousands of prophetic singers will be called forth because of this book.

—Corey Russell, Author and Speaker

Honest, instructive, and full of revelation - this book will lift you to a new level of singing the song of the Lord. I love Rachel's pursuit of the throne room and the One seated there. I also love her commitment to be rooted in her local church. Through her many years of worship leading, Rachel pours forth lessons both highly practical and deeply spiritual. With solid biblical context and raw personal stories, Rachel unfolds how we can partner with the Holy Spirit to deliver a prophetic song. "Called to Sing" has something powerful to impart to the Body of Christ in this hour – our Father is singing over us and He is letting us sing along! Prepare to grow into a singing mouthpiece of God's heart…not because you are on the worship team, but because you are a worshipper!

—R. Sonny Misar, Founder of Journey Ministries, LLC,
Director of the Radiant Network of churches
Author of *Journey to Authenticity* and *Journey to the Father*

Called to Sing is much more than another book full of information. It truly is a catalyst to unlock the wells of worship in your own heart and awaken the song you were born to sing.

—Jonathan Helser, Founder of the Cageless
Birds missional community

I am so excited for you to read *Called to Sing* by Rachel Culver! This is a time in history like none before where the Lord is stirring up the songs and the voices of all believers! This book itself is a prophetic call to this generation, and Rachel practically unpacks singing the word of the Lord. Enjoy!

—Laura Hackett Park, Worship Leader
and Songwriter at IHOP–KC

To the past, current, and future students of Radiant School of Worship, we started this school to raise up and train prophetic singers, musicians, and worship leaders. And that is who you are. You are called to sing. This book was written with you first and foremost in mind. My desire is for you to sense and believe your value and worth. You have a high calling. Sing!

Contents

Acknowledgments xi
Foreword xiii
Introduction: Called to Sing xvii

1. Every Voice 1
2. The Calling 17
3. The Levite 29
4. Prophetic Songs in the Bible 47
5. Hearing the Voice of God 61
6. Developing Biblical Language 75
7. Prophetic Song 101
8. Prophetic Songs in a Corporate Context 109
9. Partnership: Prophetic Singing and the Prophetic Musician ... 129
10. Singing on a Worship Team 143
11. Now is the Time 165

About the Author 173

Acknowledgments

Edie Mourey, I thought editors were only focused on grammar and proper sentence structure. Thank God you are much more than that. This work needed more than just your magnificent attention to detail. It needed a brilliant mother in the faith to carefully craft and package my thoughts and ideas into paragraphs and chapters of comprehensible stories and digestible information. Thank you for carrying this burden along with me these last months. Thank you for your patience and kindness in this first, official, written work of mine that isn't lyrics to a song.

Anna Asbury, my dear friend, I am so thankful for your voice in this book. You wear many hats so beautifully, and the prophetic singer hat is particularly striking on you. Thank you for the way you have poured yourself out to the Lord in worship leadership. The best is yet to come!

Jake Epperson, Thank you for giving your time and excellence to the cover design. You are a prophetic, creative artisan!

Radiant Church and Radiant City Music, thank you for your love, support and culture of family!

Thank you to Westbow Publishing, and Lindsey Sims for your expertise!

Pastor Lee and Jane Cummings, thank you for taking the risk inviting the Culvers to be part of your lives and church. What a gift your leadership and friendship has become. You have always empowered me to reach for what God has put on my heart, including this book. Thank you for your graciousness in the way you have created a safe place for me, a young leader, to put roots down and flourish. Thank you for leading the charge and preparing the way for prophetic worship.

Jordan Emmanuel, though you are only four years old, you are a prophetic musician. I see you, buddy. I see your skills. I see the gifts God has put inside you. My commitment to you is to watch you grow into the fullness God has ordained for you. I will get out of the way. I refuse to put you in a box; instead, I will let your uniqueness shine through and point people to Jesus. Thank you for sharing your momma these last months as I completed this project. I believe you will read it one day. Your momma loves you, sweet boy.

Aaliyah Mae, my beautiful, joyful songbird, I remember when you were two years old, singing and dancing onstage with a microphone to the song, "You are my Joy." It is my absolute pleasure being your momma and watching you grow. The way you sing a new song to the Lord every day and let melody and lyrics just flow out of you is provoking to your old mom. You are a prophetic singer. You are a leader. Your life is like a beacon of hope and joy, a lighthouse to those lost at sea. Thank you for sharing your momma these last months as I completed this project. I love you, my sweet baby girl.

Caleb, thank you for the gentle prodding to start writing this book. Thank you for believing in me and the countless times you had to remind me I could do it. No one but you knows the many times I needed to be encouraged to keep going and not give up. Thank you for speaking identity over me as a writer and a leader in prophetic singing. Thank you for being the best sounding board on the planet, hearing all my ideas and then helping me make sense of them. You are my favorite person. I love you.

Foreword

The book of Job is not usually where people turn in their Bibles to gain understanding of worship and prophetic singing. Years ago, however, while finishing my daily reading in Job 38, a passage that I had read many times jumped off the page to me, and I saw something that had never clearly registered with me before.

> "Where were you when I laid the foundations of the earth? Tell me, if you have understanding. Who determined its measurements—surely you know! Or who stretched the line upon it? On what were its bases sunk, or who laid its cornerstone, **when the morning stars sang together and all the sons of God shouted for joy?**" (vv. 4–7 ESV)

The Lord is calling Job to account and asks Job *where Job was* when He was crafting and creating the world out of nothing. I started thinking about Genesis 1, where it describes God creating the heavens and the earth with His words and hovering, incubating over the face of the deep by His Spirit. The earth was formless and void, but out of the chaos, God called forth order. But God's voice wasn't the only voice engaged at the beginning. It says that the *morning stars sang together and all the sons of God shouted for joy." Morning stars* is an Old Testament reference to angels and *sons of God* refers to His divine council of created beings. Both angels and sons of God were present at the dawn of creation. They provided the heavenly score of worship from whence everything created came forth. What an epic soundtrack it must have been as the heavenly hosts sang forth, building to crescendo as the will of the One took form!

I've thought long and hard about this passage in the years since. Why would God want the angelic choirs singing while He created? The only logical conclusion that I can come up with is that God loves singing. In fact, He describes Himself as the God who *sings* over us with songs of deliverance (Ps. 32:7 NIV). In fact, singing existed before God even created the heavens and the earth. It was out of an atmosphere of music and song that God called everything that is into existence by His mighty word. *"Let there be light! And there was light."* How magnificent is our God!

Songs and singing play an important role in the purposes of God played out through the lives of His people across all the pages of the Bible, from Miriam's song after the Exodus to the countless Psalms written by Israel's prophet king, David. The New Testament is no different. Paul admonishes us in Ephesians 5 to encourage one another with *"psalms, hymns and spiritual songs, singing and making melody to the Lord with your heart"* (ESV). One of God's greatest gifts to His people is song, and one of God's greatest gifts to the world is a singing Church.

Over the years, I have noticed that just as God used singing as a conduit to speak and call into being all things at the beginning, the voice of the Lord can still be heard in atmospheres of worship. Prophetic singing and *the song of the Lord* were thematic and very common to those living in ancient, biblical eras, but they are somewhat unfamiliar, even in the Church of God, due to our Western, skeptical mindsets. Every culture loves music and singing, but there is a difference that is tangible between songs about God and songs that are *from God*. I believe, in our time, God is re-awakening His Bride to hear His voice. He is raising up prophetic singers and psalmists to remind the Church that we do not serve a god who is on mute. We worship a singing God, a loving Bridegroom who wants to encourage, edify, and call out His purposes into our lives, like light out of darkness. One of those voices that I believe God has assigned to this generation to do that very thing is Rachel Culver.

I have known Rachel for many years now. I have been so inspired by her humility, hunger, and anointing that have been cultivated through years of digging wells in God's presence and serving Jesus's Church with joy. I have watched her wrestle through personal pain and yet lead a room of a thousand people or more straight to the throne room of God, declaring the comforting voice of the Father with prophetic precision. She is a modern-day Deborah, a leader and prophetic voice to the Church, calling us *all* to higher terrain in worship.

This book is the fruit of her life's calling and dedication, her personal history with the Lord, and her diligent pursuit of developing knowledge of *the perfect pitch* of the Holy Spirit's leading. I can't think of a better book on the subject available anywhere, which excites me. I believe this book will inspire a generation of worshippers and worship leaders to hear and declare phrases and choruses that capture the Father's heart.

God wants His Church in these last days to join in with the choirs of angels, heavenly hosts, and the redeemed of the Lord already gathered around His throne in heaven in one symphony of praise, as a backdrop for the new thing He is doing in the earth. You and I are called to sing the song of the Lord, out of which God will show Himself strong and mighty in our day!

I will conclude with the words from a song that Rachel and her husband, Caleb, wrote for our church family. I believe some of it was given prophetically during prayer meetings, making it even more meaningful and appropriate for this foreword. The lyrics say everything we need to know to respond to the Lord with our "yes" as He beckons us out into deeper waters of understanding and expression:

> *Creation's already singing. The rocks are ready to shout. Heaven's already declaring, but it's our turn now! It's our turn now!*

May we all embrace our own call to sing.
Pastor Lee M. Cummings
Founding Senior Pastor of Radiant Church

Introduction: Called to Sing

God is in love with the sound of your voice. No, not just that famous person's voice who pops in your head when someone says "singer." He is fascinated with *your* voice. In fact, yours is His favorite. Singing is not a spiritual gift given to a chosen few. It is a biblical command we are all to obey. And God doesn't muscle through listening to you obey the command to sing. It is His delight and deep desire to hear your voice.

Besides, you were made to sing. You were created to sing melodies and songs to the King of kings and the Lord of lords and have them move His heart. This is who you are. You ARE a singer. And more than just a singer. You were created to be a friend of God, to have a personal and intimate relationship with the God of the universe, the God who wants to speak with You. You are a singer who can hear God's voice and then respond back to Him when He speaks. This is who you are. This is who you are called to be and how you are to live your life. You are to release the testimony of Jesus wherever you go! You are a voice God wants to speak through, and you are a voice God wants to hear. You are called to sing.

Who Am I?

There are a couple things I want you to know about me.

First, **I love the presence of God**. To know Him is to experience His presence. His presence is everywhere, but my awareness and ability to sense Him are heightened in worship. I felt called to worship ministry since I was a kid. I was saved at a young age and by the grace of God have been walking with Him for 30 years. I have always felt my heart come most alive in worship. I am passionate about His presence and bringing others in through the gate of worship to experience His presence too.

I love the Word of God. Straight out of high school, I decided to attend Elim Bible Institute in Lima, New York, to continue to develop the biblical foundation I received growing up. I believe giving the Lord this first year of my independent life was a symbol of the way I wanted to live my life pursuing the knowledge of God through His Word. As my relationship with God grew, so did my love for His Word.

I am passionate about prayer. My handsome hunk of a man, Caleb, who I had been dating for three years proposed in 2005, and I moved to Missouri to join him at the International House of Prayer in Kansas City. Caleb and I were on staff there together for nearly a decade. IHOP–KC has been forerunning and leading the charge for prayer and prophetic singing as they have raised up and trained thousands to walk in their identity as intercessors and prophetic singers. It was there that I really learned about prayer, and I began operating as a prophetic singer. I would lead worship and prayer sets for hours a day, six days a week, and sing my little heart out to an empty room and, more importantly, to Jesus. These years shaped much of who I am today and my love for prayer.

I care about excellence in craft, skill, and creativity. I spent many of my adolescent years taking piano lessons and voice lessons, slowly growing in my skills. And I did the same off and on as an adult. Shortly after my time at Bible school, I decided to focus my attention on learning and growing as a worship leader and a singer. I packed my things and flew to the other side of the world to study worship and creative arts at Hillsong International Leadership College. What an experience that was! I gleaned from their excellence in worship and in songwriting, and I was blown away by the vision casting and culture setting they were able to do throughout the school as well as every Hillsong church campus.

I am a vocal coach. I want to see our singers and worship leaders equipped with the tools and skills to grow in their craft with vocal health and incredible sound.

I have had the privilege of teaching and coaching worship teams at the Forerunner Music Academy, the OneThing Internship, Desperation Leadership Academy, and the Radiant School of Worship. I spent years discipling and training singers, musicians, and worship leaders in skill as well as how to play prophetically, hearing and responding to the voice of God in worship. This is honestly one of my favorite things to do!

I love the local church. I grew up in church, and I believe in the Church. I have been leading worship in church since my teenage years and value the corporate gathering of the saints.

My family and I get to call Radiant Church in Kalamazoo, Michigan, our home. It is such a gift to be part of the Body of Christ and what God is doing on the earth. My pastors, Lee and Jane Cummings, are two of the best leaders I have ever had the privilege of working under. I get to spend a lot of my time teaching and coaching our singers as well as songwriting and leading worship.

My heart is to build God's house by nurturing, teaching, coaching, and developing the singers, musicians, and worship leaders to take their place as Levites and usher in the presence of God in our churches, cities, and nations.

Enough about me. I will share more personal stories about my own journey as we continue. Next, let's look at what you can expect from the material presented in this book.

What to Expect

Although anyone can read this book and receive from it, I did write this book with a specific reader in mind. I wrote this book for the singers who are being called and raised up in this present hour. I want to help equip those who lead other believers in worship. I see limited amounts of resources and next to zero practical tools and manuals available to instruct and encourage the voices leading us in worship, the ones called to lead the singing. It is a real calling, by the way. It is the call of the worship leader, but it is also the calling of those who lead in singing. If you're one of those individuals, then this book is for you.

As you will discover, each chapter begins with a testimony. I have compiled each testimony to highlight how God is using prophetic songs throughout the Body of Christ to minister to the saints. These testimonies come from across the United States. I hope they inspire you as they have inspired me.

At the end of every chapter, I have written a prayer. I want to encourage you from the get-go to pray these prayers aloud as I believe they will help you engage with the Lord. Use the space provided to take notes and to journal thoughts and prayers.

Following every prayer, I have included one or more prompts. These prompts are vital to getting the full effect of the book. They are here to help you engage with the text in a dynamic way.

Chapter 5 will be one of your favorites, I think. My friend and fellow prophetic singer, Anna Asbury, who has a gift with language and giving inspiration, has graciously guest authored the chapter. Her insight on hearing God's voice and the opportunities He gives us to encounter Him will be sure to cause you to set new rhythms and disciplines in your life.

I have a few recommendations as you start reading so you get the most out of the book. First, I highly recommend not rushing through the read to the finish. Take the time necessary to complete the prompts I left for you at the end of every chapter. Don't move on to the next chapter before they are done. These prompts are practical ways to apply the chapter material to your life and your singing. Take notes, journal, pray, and use this book as a workbook. Second, if you are a singer and are looking not only to practice your singing but, more specifically, your prophetic singing, I recommend also getting the audiobook as it includes instrumental music sections for you to sing with.

Worship leaders, this would be a great resource for you and the singers on your worship team. Read it together, going through the singing and non-singing prompts together in a small group! Your singers need to know they are valued and need a resource to help them grow.

Some books have incredible birth stories, like how the book was conceived in the heart of the author and the divine process of carrying the message, developing the message, and then finally getting it on paper. Well, I will tell you I never set out in my life to write a book. It was not on my bucket list. But I have been carrying this message of prophetic singing with me on my journey for a couple of decades now. And much like carrying a baby through delivery, the process of writing this book has been a real labor of love. I started this project during Covid and in the midst of the hardest year and a half of my life thus far. It is a miracle I am finally getting to write this section as my last and final piece of the book.

Prophetic singing has easily become my preoccupation: practicing it, leading it, teaching it, and raising up others to say *yes* to their calling as prophetic singers. I am passionate about this gift and the calling of prophetic singing. I am a prophetic singer, and my heart is to call you into the same calling and give you tools that will equip you as you step into your identity and calling as a prophetic singer in the house of the Lord. So, let's get started.

A Testimony

In 2011, I began to experience postpartum depression. I had never experienced depression in any form before and never understood those who had. Every night, at the exact same time, it would hit me. One day I discovered live broadcast worship sets from a ministry online. I honestly discovered a gold mine, because it was the tool that would set me free and bring joy back into my life.

They would wait on the Lord and not rush the song, enabling that song to seep deep into the soul. It was the fact that they would not only welcome, but make room for the Holy Spirit to take over, in prophetic song, adding another dimension and layer to the healing that was already taking place. It would bring the Kingdom of heaven to earth in my life because these were words directly from the Kingdom. It would cause me to long to know Him more in the secret place, because these prophetic melodies came from the secret place. It also opened up my own spiritual ears. I wondered what the source of the power behind their songs and prophetic songs was when I heard Isaiah 61:3, "Put on the garment of praise for the spirit of heaviness." I realized that I was wrestling with a spirit of heaviness and this worship, in Spirit and in truth, was replacing the heaviness with joy overflowing.

—Julie

Every Voice

There is a sound rising up from your church. Sons and daughters who know they're free. Shouting anthems of victory. —lyrics to *From This House*

God is on the move. He is doing a new thing in our day. When God does a new thing, the people of God sing a new song. When God releases deliverance, the people of God sing a new song. So, now is the time to sing!

    This new song that God is calling the Church to release is not an ambiguous or indistinct song. It's the song of freedom. It's the sound of the Body of Christ coming together in unity. It's not the sound of beautiful melodies and harmonies or the skilled sound of perfectly pitched professional voices. It is the sound of *every* voice singing and making melody. It's the sound of the Church rising up and taking her place.

The Call to All

We are *all* called to sing the new song. All of us should be prophetic singers. We are all invited to lift up our voices in praise and adoration to God and in prophetic proclamation to His people.

In the end of this age, a sound will rise out of every tribe, tongue, people, and nation. But we can join in the song now. It is a song Creation is already singing. The heavens have been declaring this song from the beginning of time. Even the rocks are getting ready to shout out the song if we don't rise up and take our place. It is our turn to sing the song!

So, let me ask you a question: Are you a singer?

Your immediate response to that question answers a lot about how you view the role of a singer. I teach a prophetic singing class at the Radiant School of Worship in Kalamazoo, Michigan, and before I get to any of my teaching content, I begin by asking a similar question: Who here can sing?

You can feel the uneasiness and insecurity in the room rise like bread in the oven. The drummers, bassists, keyboardists, and electric guitar players all know what's coming. They know I am trying to trick them, but they still can't seem to bring themselves to raise their hands. You may not be able to answer the question yourself with a clear *yes*. Perhaps you would want to offer a few qualifiers first like how it's not your profession, or you sing, *but* there are other things you do better.

> In the end of this age, a sound will rise out of every tribe, tongue, people, and nation. But we can join in the song now. It is a song Creation is already singing. The heavens have been declaring this song from the beginning of time. Even the rocks are getting ready to shout out the song if we don't rise up and take our place. It is our turn to sing the song!

Even the student singers in class have a problem raising their hands. They slowly and bashfully raise their hands only an inch or two above their heads. Even though they are enrolled in worship school as singers or they are singing onstage on a regular basis or had countless people affirm their singing gift, they still often feel funny about acknowledging that they can sing.

Let me go back to my original question: Are you a singer? Did you respond *yes* or *no*? This question is all too often accompanied by an unwelcome inner voice that tries to redefine the question to something like—what she *means* is do you think you have a good singing voice? It's the reason the musicians in my class don't raise their hands or the reason you are tempted to deflect if someone directly asks you the same or a similar question. If you think you don't have a great singing voice, you answer *no*. Right? If you think you sing well, then you don't want to seem prideful.

The answer, however, should be an immediate, definitive, resounding *yes*! You can sing. Not only can you sing, *but you are also a singer.*

Our singing God handcrafted us with a unique gift that is unspeakably precious to Him. It is our song. We all have words, worship, melody, rhythm, praise, poetry, and prophetic utterance inextricably woven into the very fabric of who we are. God didn't create any non-singers, just those who have received and activated the perfect gift God placed inside them, and those who are waiting for their song to be unlocked.

We need to be liberated from being bound up and silenced by the world's definition of what it means to be a singer. We must think of singing as a part of who we are as His people and not as something we do. We are singers.

Everyone Can Sing

We are all capable of singing. Singing in its simplest form is resonating and intoning. It's reverberating sound that often includes words. As Jesus' followers, we are *commanded* to sing. In fact, singing is one of the most commanded actions in the Bible as it's commanded over 400 times! Here are several ways we're commanded to sing: "Sing to the Lord," "Make melody in your heart," "Sing praise," "Sing a new song," "Sing unto the Lord," and "Come into His presence with singing."

There are so many other things in Scripture that are only commanded once, and that should be enough to take it seriously. But God went above and beyond to shout to us that *singing isn't optional; it is a biblical command.*

Our celebrity-obsessed, Western culture has tripped us up on this subject. We fawn over, and even worship, vocal ability. We have an overwhelming amount of incredible, beautiful, creative, and awe-inspiring singers in hundreds of genres of music. We have TV shows devoted to searching out new vocal talent because we love to elevate people with exceptional singing voices. We pay big bucks to buy their music and to hear them sing live.

Let me be clear, this is a good thing! I love hearing someone whom God has created with profound ability use the very thing the Creator designed them to use. But, because of our celebrity-obsessed culture, we have left singing to the professionals. We have gone from being participants in one of the most precious gifts to being mere spectators and onlookers of gifting and talent.

I'm not just talking about the world, either. This spectator mindset is why our churches are filled with beautiful music yet so rarely echo with the choir of voices.

It's time for a change.

Mary of Bethany

In Matthew 26:6–8, we see an invitation to give Jesus *what He wants* and not what the crowd assumes He wants. It's in the scene where Mary of Bethany broke her jar of costly perfume at the feet of Jesus as an act of worship.

> *And when Jesus was in Bethany at the house of Simon the leper, a woman came to Him having an alabaster flask of very costly fragrant oil, and she poured it on His head as He sat at the table. But when His disciples saw it, they were indignant, saying, "Why this waste? For this fragrant oil might have been sold for much and given to the poor."*

The disciples, Pharisees, and other leaders saw Mary's extravagant worship, smelled the fragrance, and instead of being moved to join in and participate, they merely watched her—watched someone else—worship

Jesus. They were spectators of a worship service that Mary was leading. The disciples were so uncomfortable with the extravagance of her display that they criticized her worship, stating she had given too much. These were *the disciples* who said this, not the "bad guy" religious Pharisees. These were the good guys, the ones who knew and loved Jesus. The disciples were the ones who would later start and lead the Church. They were like you and me.

It is a scary thing to think about showing up to a worship service and, instead of engaging in worship by using our own voices to sing, we leave it up to the "professionals" onstage. We remain silent in worship. We watch and listen as someone else pours out their alabaster jar at Jesus' feet. Our emotions are moved by these moments. We might even be fooled into thinking we were the ones who offered up the worship because we were in the room. But let me tell you, Mary was the *only one* who offered worship to Jesus in that moment. The others in the room at worst were worship critics and, at best, observers. That's it. Observers.

Oh God, let us not be mere observers of worship. Let us not smell the fragrance of another's worship and mistake it for our own. Let us not be deceived. Let not the beautiful voice from stage be the only voice that worships. Let us be a people who worship during corporate worship, that every voice would sing and every person would break open their jar of worship.

Your alabaster jar is a symbol of your life. It is a representation of everything you have wrapped up in a jar. It is your soul, your hopes, dreams, joy, and emotions. It is your hurt, pain, sadness, and mourning. It is your act of worship, your surrender. It is all that you have to give. And it is of great worth. Be like Mary who chose to offer her jar in obedient worship and was unmoved by the criticism and judgment of those around her.

Why We Don't Sing or Engage in Worship

Now that we know we always have something to offer the Lord in worship, why do we not engage? Why don't we sing and break open our alabaster jar?

Throughout the years, I have found myself battling lies from the enemy that have tried to silence my own song of praise. Let's look at four specific lies we all face at one time or another.

We Lack Skill and Confidence

"I am not a good singer. I can't follow the singers on stage. I am not musical." These statements point to our perceived lack of skill and confidence.

We have disqualified ourselves from the biblical command to sing because in our own minds the command requires a skill we lack. But God never said He wanted the skillful to sing. He wants us *all* to sing and lift our voices. He wants us to be joyful noisemakers—joyful singers!

When I was in fourth grade, I joined a Christian group called Pioneer Clubs. Pioneer Clubs are a Christian version of Boy Scouts or Girl Scouts. My first trip with a local club was a daytrip to an offsite location, which just happened to be the club leader's home. What would have been an exciting day for most ten-year-old girls filled with making homemade candles, nature walks, and collecting more club badges, for me, was one of the moments in my history that the enemy had circled on his calendar to try and sow insecurity and shut me up from my calling as a worshipper and as a singer.

We had a break between each club activity, and eight of us girls were sitting in the living room, passing around a karaoke microphone, giggling and singing our little hearts out to the music. It was finally my turn to sing, and I can't remember what song it was I was singing, but I can vividly remember the words that flew out of the most popular girl's mouth as she snatched the microphone out of my hand. She smirked as she said, "Whoa, that was awful! Give me the microphone before you hurt our ears."

Now, let me tell you, this girl was blonde, blue-eyed, and loved by everyone. So, what she said mattered. In that moment, I figured what she said must be true, so I thought I needed to stop singing in front of people immediately. I had never known insecurity related to my voice before that moment. I went from being a confident ten-year-old little girl to questioning my voice and my love for singing.

Look back on your own life for a minute. Was there a time when you loved to sing? Was there a time when you were uninhibited when you sang? Did you have a moment like mine when someone said something that caused you to be insecure about your voice or ability to sing?

I remember in music class in fourth and fifth grades, both the girls and boys all loved to sing. We enjoyed singing. In fourth grade, we sang the "Carol of the Bells" for our school Christmas concert, and everyone smiled and belted out every word. Then in fifth grade, we were tasked with multiple songs from a Christian Christmas musical which we absolutely crushed with confidence and genuine enjoyment. But then something changed in sixth grade. It was as if a switch were flipped, and only a few enjoyed music class anymore. Most of my classmates suddenly became timid and wouldn't sing loud or strong anymore. In fact, from that point on, most of my fellow classmates avoided singing altogether. No one sang in choir, few sang in worship during chapel, and absolutely no one sang just for fun. It was like singing was no longer cool.

Maybe you have been held back by a lie or word curse spoken over you years ago. Maybe someone told you that you couldn't sing. Maybe, when your voice started maturing and changing, you believed that meant it was time to stop singing because you had less control. Or maybe your voice cracked, and your friends laughed at you enough to silence the voice God gave you.

Insecurity crept into this area of your life that used to bring you joy. Perhaps the fear of man has locked you up in a cage. *But no more!*

It is time to sing. It is time to break your agreement with those lies and word curses spoken over your singing voice. It is time to sing a melody that brings you joy. Your Father in heaven longs to hear you sing to Him. It brings Him joy. It is your time to sing again.

We Don't Feel Like It

This might be the excuse we find ourselves operating in the most. We are so driven and controlled by our emotions. Often, we let our emotions dictate what we do and what we don't do. We don't feel like doing something, so we don't do it.

Have you ever felt any of these feelings when you showed up on a Sunday morning to church?

- "I just don't feel like singing."
- "I am too tired."
- "I am too mad to sing."
- *"I am not in the mood."*

Our emotions are part of what makes up our soul. Our soul is comprised of our mind, will, and emotions. All three parts of our soul must submit to our spirit. We want the spirit within us to be the one in the driver's seat in our inner lives. Despite our feelings and what we want to do in a moment, we sing and worship because our spirit comes alive when we do. We choose to sing, and in doing so, our souls submit to Jesus and to the Holy Spirit.

In Romans 8, Paul talks about walking according to the Spirit and not the flesh. When we walk according to the Spirit, our emotions, along with the rest of our flesh, is submitted to the Spirit.

When we choose to sing and lift our voices in worship when we don't feel like it, suddenly we begin to feel like it. Singing in worship will bring us to a place where our mood shifts. Our negative feelings are neutralized, and we can feel our emotions begin to experience something different.

We need to follow the example that the Psalms lay out for us. Over and over again, we see this phrase, "Bless the Lord O my soul." Psalm 103:1–2 says, *"Bless the Lord O my soul and all that is within me bless His holy Name. Bless the Lord O my soul and forget not all his benefits."* Command your soul to praise the Lord. Praising and singing to Him have nothing to do with your feelings. The Scripture doesn't say, "When you feel like it, go ahead and bless the Lord," or "When your soul wants to, you should totally bless the Lord." No! We command our souls to praise. Praise should transcend our feelings.

We Don't Believe God Really Wants Our Worship

This thought or lie comes down to our value. We don't know who we are and what our worship means to God. We don't realize that our worship moves His heart more than anything. He loves the sound of our voices and the fragrance of our worship. Our individual voices are unique. Your voice and sound and worship are uniquely yours. Do you believe God is looking and longing for your voice to worship Him? Or have you believed one of the lies listed below?

- "My voice doesn't matter."
- "I don't have a voice."
- "My worship is too weak."
- "What I have to give is not enough."
- "My worship isn't valuable."

We begin to believe that God truly desires our worship when we understand He loves our worship as weak as it may be because He loves us.

My daughter is eight years old and has a deep love for art. She has been consistently drawing all kinds of pictures of people and animals. I can't tell you how many times she has given one of these drawings to me as a gift. She will walk upstairs, leaving her little artist desk, and hand me her newest creation and say, "Look, Momma, I made this for you!" Imagine me, as her parent, scoffing at the gift and telling her I didn't want any drawings from her until they were perfect masterpieces. "Don't even bother giving me anything unless it's perfect." We would never say something like that to our children. We *love* the small gifts they give. I have heard some parents receive bugs and other icky insects as gifts from their adventurous little sons or daughters. These parents have the opportunity to see the beautiful, giving heart of their child wanting to love them through the offering of a gift, even if the gift is crawling!

> **He enjoys our worship. He enjoys *your* worship. Do not withhold that which our God greatly desires. You are enough. Your song and your voice please Him, and He loves to hear you worship.**

God sees our weak and imperfect worship, and oh, how it moves His heart. He enjoys our worship. He enjoys *your* worship. Do not withhold that which our God greatly desires. You are enough. Your song and your voice please Him, and He loves to hear you worship.

We Don't Believe He Is Worthy of Our Worship

Is God who He says He is? Do we believe He truly is a good God deserving of worship?

I have seen friends who love God with all their hearts, the ones who sang the loudest and worshipped with their whole beings, begin to question the goodness of God. Years brought hardship, pain, or trauma, and they found themselves slowly walking away from their faith. One week they showed up at church and couldn't bring themselves to sing the lyrics to "Reckless Love," where it says, "You have been so, so good to me." They don't believe that line anymore.

Many times, the progression into this lie works subconsciously. People who have been believers just slowly stop singing because they are no longer convinced that God is good. Life got tough, and they blamed God. I'm not talking about them shaking their fist at God and walking away from church, although that can happen. I am talking about a slow and subtle backpedal from worship as they question if God is really God, and if He is God, they begin to doubt that He is good.

The truth is our God is good. He is worthy beyond measure. He loves us. He is for us. And He deserves all of our praise and worship. But our belief in this gets shaken when we blame Him for any and every disappointment, unmet expectation, pain, and every other negative thing that happens in our lives.

What Happens When We Sing in Worship?

We were made to glorify God. When we sing, God is glorified. We were created to worship Him. We are fulfilling our primary calling as human beings when we worship Him.

God said in Isaiah 66:1, *"Heaven is my throne, and the earth is my footstool. Where is the house you will build for me? Where will my resting place be?"* We can give God a resting place on the earth. In fact, we become God's resting place—not our church buildings, but the people of God gathered in worship.

Psalm 22:3 says that God inhabits the praises of His people. When we worship, we create the place for Him to dwell and live. When we worship in our cars, in our homes, or at our workplaces, we are inviting His presence to come and inhabit our praise. Most translations use the word *enthrone* in Psalm 22:3. God is enthroned on our praise. He is given the highest place.

When we sing in worship, we are obeying God's command.

When we sing in worship, we are speaking truth over our own lives, families, situations, and souls. We are encouraged, uplifted, and given clear perspective when we worship. Our countenances change when we sing. We are ushered into a place of joy and peace when we worship.

Worship displaces darkness and principalities. There is a reason King Jehoshaphat sent the worshippers out in front of his army to defeat the enemy (see 2 Chron. 20:21).

Psalm 33:3

Psalm 33:3 says, *"Sing to Him a new song; play skillfully, and shout for joy."* The first half of this verse is the command for *all* to sing to Jesus. It is a command to sing the new song. When God does a new thing, we sing a new song of worship to Him.

I feel very passionately about the entirety of the Body of Christ stepping into our identity as singers and noisemakers before the Lord. Psalm 100 says, *"Make a joyful **noise** to the Lord **all** you lands!"* (AMPC). This is where our hearts come alive. It is here, in the place of worship, that we position our hearts in His presence and are transformed into His image.

In Psalm 150:6, the call is for *everyone* who has breath to praise the Lord! Praise Him with your voice and with your own mouth. Do it out loud! Remember this command does not require skill. So go for it! Don't hold back. Don't be the guy in the chair with his arms folded in worship. It is not time to sit on the sidelines and let your brothers and sisters in the faith break open their worship without you. You have everything you need to lift up your voice.

Sing! Sing the song of your brother. Sing the song of your sister. Sing your own song to the Lord. Sing the words on the screen. Sing the

Scriptures. Sing language out of the overflow of your own heart. Make melody and combine it with worshipful phrases straight to His heart.

To the Skillful

Maybe someday I will write a book solely on the command to sing. Surely there is enough content to fill many books. But this book is written specifically for the ones to whom God has given the second command in Psalm 33:3, "*Sing to Him a new song;* ***play skillfully.* . . .**" This command to be skillful in worship is not one God has given for everyone. It is for the leaders of the songs; the worship leaders, singers, musicians, songwriters, band directors, and others who are called to be Levites in the house of God. Some have this role as an occupation, but so many more are called to do this in an intentional way on worship teams, prayer room teams, and other leadership avenues where worship is happening in a corporate expression.

I have written this book as a manual and as a guide for singers who are called to sing and want to grow in their gifting, skill, and anointing. It is my desire to give you tools and information I wish I had when I first started my journey as a prophetic singer. My goal is to be vulnerable and transparent. I have included at least one prompt at the end of each chapter, and I strongly encourage you to engage and participate in each prompt. Some will take more thought and energy than others, but I believe these prompts and exercises are a massive part of what I want to communicate and help you receive from our time together through your reading this book. I have been using these prompts myself and with our students and other small groups for years and have seen the growth and fruit they produce. I have also left multiple journaling spaces for you throughout the book. Take advantage of these spaces. Let them awaken your creativity and use them to write songs, dialogue with Jesus, draw, doodle, or make notes.

I believe with all my heart that God is raising up prophetic singers and musicians across the globe to lead the people of God in singing the new song. May this book be a helpful tool as you grow and develop as a prophetic singer.

Closing Prayer

Pray this prayer with me over yourself. It may help to read it aloud.

Father,
I respond to Your call to sing. I confess I have been silent. I have let how I feel dictate whether I sang my song of worship to You. I repent for allowing others to break open their alabaster jar of worship before You while I sat back, being entertained by the music. I now recognize my role as a worshipper and as a singer. I choose to worship. I will choose to sing. I believe You are worthy!

I break my agreement with every lie I have believed in the past about my voice and my song. I will not be silent. I will offer up a joyful noise to You!

Would You fill my mouth with praise? Will You cause it flow out of me like never before? Would You inspire songs of praise to be on my tongue at all times? I take my place as a singer and worshipper before You. Amen.

Prompt

Sing! That's right. Find a place where you feel comfortable and where there are less distractions and potential interruptions. Choose your current favorite worship song or a worship song that you know by heart. Open up your mouth and begin to sing it!
Slow down and don't sing it too fast. Find the correct tempo and really sing the song. Give it your all.
Once you have sung the whole song from start to finish, tell yourself aloud, "I can sing!" Go ahead, say it! "I can sing!"

Journal whatever comes to you regarding this prompt. What were the lies that came up against you before, during, and after the exercise?

Now ask the Lord what He thought of your voice. Ask Him how He felt when you sang to Him. What is the truth?

A Testimony

The Lord encountered me through a prophetic song in a prayer meeting. I didn't plan to attend this prayer meeting, but because of several random factors, I found myself there to help resolve an issue.

As I was leaving to go home, I felt the strong compulsion to stay and listen to the worship team on the stage. So, I stayed. The entire time I had been in there earlier, the worship team was just playing instrumental music. But as soon as I sat down, the singer started to sing a spontaneous chorus:

> *In the moment of your weakness*
> *When you're expecting a harsh word*
> *I'll reach in with My kindness*
> *And give you what you don't deserve.*
> *Battered by accusation*
> *I'll be the one to tend your hurt*
> *I'll reach in with My kindness*
> *And give you what you don't deserve.*

*I instantly started weeping. I felt so many emotions at once, but the thing that stood out in that moment was that I **could** be vulnerable and show those emotions. God was a Father, not reluctantly taking care of me, but actively looking for ways to show me His love, kindness, and grace. In that moment, I felt the freedom to just be a weak and broken child yet be lifted into the arms of my merciful Father.*

I never heard them sing that chorus again. To this day, I randomly remember it, and every time I sing it, I cry and think of that moment where I felt the Love of the Father.

—Sean

The Calling

The calling of a prophetic singer is like the calling of every believer. It is first and foremost a calling to intimacy with Jesus. Prophetic singers are lovers of Jesus first. Before we are anything else and before we do anything—sing any song or prophesy—we are simply ones who love Jesus with all our heart, soul, mind, and strength. Our personal relationship with Jesus is more than a side project or hobby. It is everything because He is everything.

We can't be who we were made to be and fulfill our calling if we don't know who we are. We discover who we are when we know who Jesus is and understand our relationship to Him. He defines us. He tells us who we are. His voice is what calls us into our being and into our place. His voice that commands the morning is the same voice that declares our identity over us. We must first know this Man Jesus. We must understand we belong to Him. He then becomes our one desire, our obsession. Then we can

> **The calling of a prophetic singer is like the calling of every believer. It is first and foremost a calling to intimacy with Jesus. Prophetic singers are lovers of Jesus first.**

walk in our primary calling to have a real and authentic relationship with Him.

Psalm 27:4

The psalmist David understood this idea of God being his chief desire when he wrote Psalm 27:4, which says, *"One thing I have desired of the Lord, that will I seek: That I may dwell in the house of the Lord all of the days of my life, to behold the beauty of the Lord, and to enquire in His temple"* (NKJV). Let's look at each phrase of this verse as it relates to our primary calling.

"One Thing I Have Desired"

Whenever I think about this phrase, I am immediately transported back to 2001 when I first heard the song "Obsession" by Delirious?. I was at a summer Christian youth camp called Camp Shiloh, and a teenage boy about my age was kneeling, weeping on the chapel stage with a microphone in his hand as he sang the lyrics, "My heart burns for You." He sang this phrase over and over and over again. He sang it a few times with surety and strength in his voice, and then his voice would quiver and shake as he sang, as he was overcome by his emotions and deep affection for Jesus. I felt the intensity of his heart toward Jesus. He wept as if no one else were in the room.

I felt provoked, watching this teenage boy. It was like nothing else in the world mattered to him except telling Jesus how much he loved Him. I forgot to mention that this worship set was taking place during a time in the camp schedule called "Skills Class." The campers would scatter to classes for soccer, basketball, swimming, archery, painting, chess, volleyball, dodgeball, and more. There was one other "class" you could take during this time, and it was simply a worship and prayer

> **Jesus is our greatest calling. The pursuit of God is what we were all made for: to seek Him with our whole hearts, to be obsessed with Him.**

time led by campers. This was the least attended class in all the camp. And I was just walking by the outdoor worship chapel on my way to an exhilarating canoeing class when the scene I described above unfolded. I never made it to my canoe that day. I stood in the back of that chapel and was provoked to desire Jesus like this fellow camper did.

Fast forward five years, and this fellow teenage camper became my husband! We have been married now for fifteen years, and Caleb is still constantly provoking me by his deep passion and desire for Jesus. Before anything else, he is committed to loving, serving, and worshipping our God. I am thankful for his consistent example to me, my kids, and our community of what it looks like to desire the Lord.

Jesus must become our One Thing. He must become first, and He must become the Only Thing. There are so many things we can give our time to, so many pursuits that are desiring our attention. What are you obsessed with? Is it the latest and greatest technology Apple has to offer? (Yes, I am talking about your phone!) Are you obsessed with your image or how people view you? Is your greatest desire to become an influencer and achieve status and fame? Or are you obsessed with your career, success, and advancing up the ranks? Maybe you are obsessed with singing and sounding the best, or maybe you're obsessed with ministry?

We cannot be obsessed with multiple things—only one thing. What is your one thing? What is the one thing you desire?

Jesus is our greatest calling. The pursuit of God is what we were all made for: to seek Him with our whole hearts, to be obsessed with Him. Jesus is our Source and our exceedingly Great Reward. He is our everything. As God said to Abraham, *"I am your shield, your very great reward"* (Gen. 15:1).

"That Will I Seek"

Seeking is an active word. We pursue. We seek after that which we desire. When we desire something, we are diligent in our quest. We don't give up easily. We don't get sidetracked or derailed. There is a spiritual principle in Matthew 7:7–11 I want us to look at:

> *"Ask, and it will be given to you; **seek, and you will find;** knock, and it will be opened to you. For everyone who asks receives, and he who seeks finds, and to him who knocks it will be opened. Or what man is there among you who, if his son asks for bread, will give him a stone? Or if he asks for a fish, will he give him a serpent? If you then, being evil, know how to give good gifts to your children, how much more will your Father who is in heaven give good things to those who ask Him!" (NKJV)*

When we set our hearts to seek after Jesus, our One Thing, this spiritual principle in Matthew 7 tells us that we find Him. We seek Him, not because He is hiding from us, but because He wants to be found by us. When we recognize our need for Him, He becomes our greatest pursuit, our most important round of hide-and-go-seek.

"That I May Dwell in the House of the Lord"

When we spend our time in pursuit of the One Thing, we develop our relationship with God. Dwelling in the house of the Lord refers simply to being with Him. This needs to be our desire, our primary focus, and the goal of our lives. Spending time with someone is the best way to get to know that person. I love reading books about God. I learn so much about who He is through other people's stories, personal encounters, as well as their teaching and revelation of Jesus. But reading about someone does not make a relationship. It is not dwelling in His presence. We dwell in His house by being with Him ourselves.

We also dwell in His house by spending time in the house of God, the church, and gathering corporately with believers to praise and to worship. We posture our hearts so that we never leave the place of His presence. No matter where we may be—at home, at church, in the car, at work, or anywhere—we can dwell in His house. This is communion. We live and stay in this place, taking up residency in His presence and choosing never to leave. John 15 brings us this language: abiding in the vine. We make our home in Him.

"To Behold the Beauty of the Lord"

It takes time to behold the Lord's beauty. Beholding is not glancing or peeking. It is gazing. To gaze is to stare and take time. Gazes are long. You gaze when you don't want to miss a thing. Imagine rounding a corner and seeing the most epic of sunsets, the wonder of shade after shade of oranges, pinks, and purples taking over the evening sky. What do you do? You drop everything and stare at it. You sigh deeply, inhale, and take in every color. You slow down and feel the warm breeze on your face. You let yourself get caught up in the wonder and beauty of the evening sky.

God's beauty is wrapped up in every part of who He is as well as everything that He does. We can never run out of aspects of His beauty to gaze upon and be taken up in the wonder of it.

"To Inquire in His Temple"

Dialogue, communication, and prayer are all part of building a relationship with God. Asking Him questions and hearing His answers are necessary for understanding His heart, ways, and mind.

We are to be ones who spend time in His presence. Communication is what makes a relationship. It can be spoken language, written language, emotional language; sometimes it's simply groanings or weeping when we don't know what to say.

God desires relationship with us. Relationship requires two-way communication. It is talking to God and listening for His response. Engage in dialogue with God, not just your monologue of all the things you need, or all the prayer requests you have. Pray those things, yes, but then listen because He wants to talk back to you. Ask Him questions. Inquire of the Lord. Be in His presence and let Him speak. Give God room, time, and space to communicate to your heart.

Every human being was made for the presence of God. David tapped into this truth and built his entire tabernacle upon it. He made the presence of God accessible and open. Up until that point, the Holy of Holies from Moses' tabernacle was not breached but only once a year by the high priest. Today, we have complete, immediate, and continuous access to the presence of God. When Jesus died, the temple veil leading into the Holy of Holies was torn as a perfect demonstration of what Jesus' death meant. Humanity then had access to the Holy of Holies, the presence of God through Jesus Christ.

The tabernacle of His presence is no longer in David's tabernacle, the temple, or stationary in a church building. The presence of God is with man, and our access to Him is always present. We have the capability to spend every day in His presence. This is our calling, to simply be with Him. As the Westminster Shorter Catechism said, "Man's chief end is to glorify God and enjoy Him forever."

Psalm 84

Psalm 84:10 says, *"Better is one day in your courts than a thousand elsewhere."* This song was written by the sons of Korah. The psalm was written during the time of David's tabernacle. The people of God would take a pilgrimage to Jerusalem and to the tabernacle. The presence of God during that time was hosted in a tent. So, the journey to the courts of the Lord was documented in Psalm 84, and you can feel the desire of the sons of Korah to be in the presence of the Lord.

I encourage you to read Psalm 84 through the lens of it being a documentation of the journey to the presence of God. You can sense the longing and anticipation of being back in His presence.

Here is Psalm 84 in its entirety:

> *How lovely is your dwelling place, Lord Almighty! My soul yearns, even faints, for the courts of the Lord; my heart and my flesh cry out for the living God. Even the sparrow has found a home, and the swallow a nest for herself, where she may have her young—a place near your altar, Lord Almighty, my King and my God. Blessed are those who dwell in your house; they are ever praising you. Blessed are those whose strength is in you, whose hearts are set on pilgrimage. As they pass through the Valley of Baka, they make it a place*

of springs; the autumn rains also cover it with pools. They go from strength to strength, till each appears before God in Zion. Hear my prayer, Lord God Almighty; listen to me, God of Jacob. Look on our shield, O God; look with favor on your anointed one. Better is one day in your courts than a thousand elsewhere; I would rather be a doorkeeper in the house of my God than dwell in the tents of the wicked. For the Lord God is a sun and shield; the Lord bestows favor and honor; no good thing does he withhold from those whose walk is blameless. Lord Almighty, blessed is the one who trusts in you.

Holy unto the Lord

First Peter 2:9 reads, *"But you are a chosen people, a royal priesthood, a holy nation, God's special possession, that you may declare the praises of Him who called you out of darkness into his wonderful light."* As the people of God, we are called to be holy unto the Lord. Just as Israel was a people set apart by God, we too are His chosen people as we have been grafted or adopted into His family. We have been set apart to live lives holy unto Him. When we fall in love with Jesus, our desires change, and we desire to live holy, consecrated lives.

> *Now in a great house there are not only vessels of gold and silver but also of wood and clay, some for honorable use, some for dishonorable. Therefore, if anyone cleanses himself from what is dishonorable, he will be a vessel for honorable use, set apart as holy, useful to the master of the house, ready for every good work. (2 Timothy 2:20–21 ESV)*

Holiness matters. Now is not the time for our worship teams to be on stage during worship but then MIA during the sermons and living for themselves six days a week. If we are leading others in worship, we are leading them in all areas. Our personal lives outside the four walls of the church matter. How we live our lives when no one is looking matters. Jesus calls us to live holy lives. He asks us to follow Him. We need to have a relationship with Jesus. We need to be growing in our relationship with Jesus. And as this relationship grows, we will become more like Him. As worship leaders, singers, musicians, and others that serve on stage in prayer meetings, church services, youth sets, and the like, we are called to be holy as He is holy.

Closing Prayer

Pray this prayer with me over yourself. It may help to read it aloud.

Jesus,
Thank You that, before we are called to anything else, we are called to be close to You. You are our greatest calling and our highest reward. May we continue this journey of knowing You and loving You. Grant us greater fervor and passion for Your name. Jesus, we want to be obsessed with You. We want Your name to be on our lips. We want to be Your friend.

May every other love and every other thing fall to the wayside. We repent for placing other things above our pursuit of You. We repent of neglecting our relationship with You.

Today, we give You first place. We give you preeminence. Take it. Become our Obsession. Become our One Thing.

We confess You are all we need. Let us be preoccupied by Your presence, inundated with Your love, and captivated by Your beauty.

We say yes to our primary calling. We say yes to love You with our whole heart. We say yes to a lifetime of pursuing You and being loved by You.
Amen.

Prompt

Take some time and think about your relationship with Jesus. I want you to ask yourself the questions that follow. Write down your response here or in your journal. Try not to simply write down the correct answers. Instead, write down what has been the truth in your life recently.

What is the "one thing" in your life right now?

What are you obsessed with? Is it your career, ministry, or favorite hobby?

What takes up the majority of your free time?

What takes up the majority of your thought life?

A Testimony

I'll never forget that night in November 2019 and where I was, which was actually at home during a live streamed service. I love that the Spirit of the Lord is not governed by physical time or place. He's alive and moving!

I'll never forget the exact words that were sung in that moment because like a wave they immediately crashed over me, and I was under. The words were:

> *With no strength left to muster*
> *I finally come in weakness*
> *You're worthy of so much more*
> *But here's my broken pieces*
> *You're worthy Jesus*
> *We fill the room with the fragrance of our worship*
> *We break it open*
> *We break it open*
> *We fill the room with the fragrance of our worship*
> *We break it open*
> *We break it open*

The Lord seared these words on my heart that night. Like Miriam's song in Exodus, this song, out of a place of vulnerability, also became my song and not just my song; it became "the song" that the Lord was ultimately glorified and magnified through because of a deep revelation released that became to me something I could take hold of and be changed by.

I had to "grow up" early because of a fragmented, broken, and dysfunctional home and upbringing, which really laid a foundation of doing things in my own strength. The Father's love through Jesus Christ encountered me and changed me later in my young adult years, and there began a journey of allowing Jesus to break old foundations and rebuild my heart. I have been walking with Jesus for over 20 years now and that process never ends, but that time in 2019 was a monumental moment for me walking in a new freedom that honestly started a journey of seeing and allowing the Lord to rebuild me because I was making a decision to fully empty myself and embrace my weakness. He had been breaking that off me layer by layer year after year, and this was the moment I had the eyes of faith to see it, hear it, and embrace it.

I feel like that one moment, though it was no more than 5 minutes, with that prophetic song had a ripple effect on me. It released truth and power for me to receive, and the lasting effects continue to ripple. The song was the drop that caused the ripple, and ripples sometimes even become waves.

—Kendra

The Levite

Back in 2010–2011, the International House of Prayer in Kansas City (IHOP–KC) was in the middle of an awakening. The Holy Spirit was showing up in a tangible way and touching lives. It was a powerful year of testimony after testimony of emotional healing, salvations, life transformation, and even some physical healings as well. Lives were being set free from years of self-hatred, shame, false ideas of who God was, and lies about their own identities. We were holding six-hour worship and prayer meetings Wednesday through Saturday, and each service was packed! During this time, I was being healed from lies I had been believing for years about who I was and what my identity was in Christ. One of the calls on my life that was solidified during this time was the call to be a Levite.

One evening, I was in my kitchen doing the dishes after one of our six-hour worship nights. As I stood there, a song from Handel's *Messiah* sprung into my spirit. It is the song called, "And He Shall Purify the Sons of Levi." If you have never heard of or listened to Handel's *Messiah*, I encourage you to give it a listen on a rainy day.

Purifying the Levite

Handel's *Messiah* is an oratorio (like an opera) written by George Handel back in 1742. The first act consists of prophecies of Jesus' first coming. The second act contains prophecies of his death and burial. The third and final act include prophecies of his resurrection and second coming. This piece of music released prophetic declarations of the Jewish Messiah, Jesus, the Savior of the World.

Back in my kitchen, I put on the song and listened to the beautifully sung rendition of Malachi 3:3—*"And he shall purify the sons of Levi, and purge them as gold and silver, that they may offer unto the Lord an offering in righteousness"* (KJV). I began to cry as I felt the Lord speak to me, "This is what I am doing with you in this season of your life. I am taking you through a process of purification. I am refining and purifying you. You are a Levite. You were made to worship, and you will lead others to do the same." The process to refine and purify is through fire, by the way.

> You are not just a singer; you are a valued member of the team. You are a Levite. Your voice matters, and your voice counts.

I am sharing this story for a few reasons. Obviously, as previously stated, this moment was the moment God spoke to me and confirmed the call on my life to be a modern-day Levite. Beyond that, Handel's *Messiah* is a modern-day example of prophetic singing. These performers were singing prophecies straight out of the Bible. Every Christmas I try to go to see the oratorio live in a concert hall. And each time, I am blown away by the way in which the testimony of Jesus goes forth. Every single song in the *Messiah* is straight, word-for-word Scripture. Every song is a prophecy pointing to Jesus.

When Act Three begins and the alto soloist sings, "I Know That My Redeemer Liveth," I cannot help but look around the room and pray that the Word of the Lord would awaken hearts to see the truth and majesty of Jesus, who is alive and madly in love with them as the prophetic song declares.

So, What Is a Levite?

The term *Levite* refers to a person who is from the tribe of Levi. In the Old Testament, God assigned the role of priest to this tribe. The Levites were set apart by God and served the nation of Israel.

God anointed Bezaleel (more about him in Chapter 9) to craft the tabernacle of Moses. In Moses' tabernacle, the first priests were Aaron and his sons. Aaron was of the tribe of Levi. As priests in Moses' tabernacle, Aaron and his sons would run the daily, weekly, and yearly sacrifices offered to God on behalf of the people and maintain the tabernacle. They were teachers of the law and functioned as gatekeepers. Once a year on the day of atonement, the high priest would enter the Holy of Holies to make a sacrifice on behalf of all the Israelites.

I want to highlight the role of the Levites during the reign of King David when he set up the tabernacle of David in a tent outside his palace and in his backyard. His administration hired 288 singers (Levites) who were trained in singing skillfully to the Lord and 4,000 musicians, also Levites, to play instruments (see 1 Chron. 25). These Levites rotated and maintained a 24/7 schedule of praise and worship in the tent.

To say King David took the role of singer in the house of God as a position with little importance would be very far from the truth. These singers were given a high honor and were respected members of the nation of Israel. They were valued greatly and were the voices that sang the Psalms for the first time. They were taken care of financially and had their other responsibilities removed so they could focus on their task of singing in David's tabernacle.

Your Value

If you are someone who sings on the weekends in your church or in a local house of prayer or maybe sings on a youth team, you are valued greatly in the Kingdom of God. You are not just a singer; you are a valued member of the team. You are a Levite. Your voice matters, and your voice counts.

My husband, Caleb, and I have travelled and have consulted for worship leaders and worship teams at different churches, and we emphasize the need for churches to create cultures where the role of the singer is valued. I have seen too many singers who just show up for rehearsal, having not rehearsed prior. I have seen too many rehearsals where the singers were ignored and not given constructive feedback. I have seen worship team cultures where the musicians form strong bonds, but the singers are left on the outskirts of the community. I have heard things like, "Oh, they are just background vocalists. They don't need to come to rehearsals. We have their mics down in the house anyway."

Your voice matters. What you bring to the team is invaluable, and the team would be lost without you. Thank you for your service and for the way you pour yourself out time and time again in worship services.

It's time to rise up and know your worth. Hold your head high and lead us into worship using that voice the Lord bestowed upon you. Arrive for practices and rehearsals with lyrics, melodies, and harmonies memorized. Come to worship services with the mentality that you are leading the people of God into worship, because you are!

The Installment of the Musicians and Singers

In 1 Chronicles 16, the ark of the covenant finally made its way safely to Jerusalem where King David had set up a tent for it. Verse four states, *"And he appointed some of the Levites to minister before the ark of the Lord, to commemorate, to thank, and to praise the Lord God of Israel"* (NKJV). Let's look at this verse phrase by phrase to better understand the role and function of the Levites in David's tabernacle.

They Were Appointed

All members of the tribe of Levi were Levites, but not all Levites were musicians, singers, and worship leaders. The Levites had numerous jobs and roles that they fulfilled as a tribe. Only some were appointed by King David to minister in the tabernacle as prophetic singers, musicians, and worship leaders.

In the first chapter of this book, we talked about everyone being called to sing and worship. It is what we are all created to do. This does not mean that every Christian is supposed to get onstage in a leadership capacity and lead worship. God appoints only some to lead.

They Were Submitted to Authority

First Chronicles 25:6 tells us something about these musicians, singers, and worship leaders:

> *They were all under the direction of their father in the music in the house of the Lord with cymbals, harps, and lyres for the service of the house of God. Asaph, Jeduthun, and Heman were under the order of the king. (ESV)*

This verse is more important than you may realize at first glance. When I read this verse, I see an authority structure. Each Levite was submitted to authority. Each musician and singer was submitted to the authority of their respective fathers: Asaph, Jeduthun, or Heman. Out of those three, Asaph was given the role of chief musician, so we know he was leading Jeduthun and Heman. Then those three leaders were also under the authority of the king.

The musicians, singers, and worship leaders were aware of who was in charge and who was submitting to whom. It was clear enough and important enough for it to find its way into Scripture, anyway. It is so important for us in the church to be submitted to authority. Jesus is our ultimate authority, but we are under the leadership of our church as well. God has placed shepherds and leaders among us to lead us and to cover us as we minister to the Body of Christ.

Worship leaders, it is important that you are submitted to the leadership and vision of the senior pastor of your church. Your pastor is a God-appointed leader in your life.

Singers and musicians on the worship team, it is important that you are submitted to the worship pastor or worship leader you are serving. You are not meant to be a rogue talent doing your own thing. You are, however, a member of the Body of Christ. You are a valuable part of a team. Your ideas, goals, and plans should be submitted to the leadership structure of which you are a part.

When you are submitted to authority, you can be bold in your expression and in your messaging because you are walking under that authority. Your confidence will grow as you lead from a place of humility, allowing leaders to cover you and speak into your ministry. Leaders don't exist to hold you back. Leaders exist to train you up and cover you in your ministry as you step out.

They Were Skilled

The ones that King David appointed were skilled as 1 Chronicles 25:1–6 tells us:

> *Moreover David and the captains of the army separated for the service some of the sons of Asaph, of Heman, and of Jeduthun, who should prophesy with harps, stringed instruments, and cymbals. And the number of the* **skilled** *men performing their service was: Of the sons of Asaph: Zaccur, Joseph, Nethaniah, and Asharelah; the sons of Asaph were under the direction of Asaph, who prophesied according to the order of the king. Of Jeduthun, the sons of Jeduthun: Gedaliah, Zeri, Jeshaiah, Shimei, Hashabiah, and Mattithiah, six, under the direction of their father Jeduthun, who prophesied with a harp to give thanks and to praise the Lord. Of Heman, the sons of Heman: Bukkiah, Mattaniah, Uzziel, Shebuel, Jerimoth, Hananiah, Hanani, Eliathah, Giddalti, Romamti-Ezer, Joshbekashah, Mallothi, Hothir, and Mahazioth. All these were the sons of Heman the king's seer in the words of God, to exalt his horn. For God gave Heman fourteen sons and three daughters. All these were*

*under the direction of their father for the music in the house of the Lord, with cymbals, stringed instruments, and harps, for the service of the house of God. Asaph, Jeduthun, and Heman were under the authority of the king. So the number of them, with their brethren who were instructed in the songs of the Lord, all who were **skillful**, was two hundred and eighty-eight. (NKJV)*

Asaph, Heman, and Jeduthun were the three main leaders of the singers and musicians, and Asaph held the position of the chief musician, as I've mentioned before. These men were leaders, skilled at playing their instruments and leading choirs and bands. Asaph and Heman were also skillful songwriters, writing and contributing some of the psalms. King David wrote some of his psalms with Jeduthun in mind to lead the vocal choirs and the singing because of Jeduthun's skill and anointing in singing (see Ps. 39; 62; 77). Jeduthun was also a skilled harpist.

These men were skilled as prophetic musicians. Heman was called a seer in the words of God. A seer is someone who sees by the Spirit in the spiritual realm. It is a specific prophetic gift. Asaph, Heman, and Jeduthun along with their sons would prophesy with different instruments. Most likely, they all could play multiple instruments.

Before the opportunity even existed to play their instrument in the tabernacle of David, they had been practicing their skills as musicians. They had been learning to prophesy. They grew up learning the skills of their fathers. They were a family of musicians, trained from a young age to sing, play instruments, and prophesy.

They were not looking for a platform. The platform they would eventually have didn't even exist during their formative years. As they were growing up, the ark of the covenant was in enemy territory. It was during a time in their nation's history when Moses' tabernacle was without the presence of God and before David's tabernacle existed.

These musicians, singers, and worship leaders just said *yes* to the calling on their lives to minister in song to the Lord. They served faithfully for years, becoming excellent and skilled singers and musicians. They studied the Word of God, which at that time was only the Pentateuch (the first five books of the Bible). When the time came, they were ready, and they became leaders in the house of God. Before the job was glamorous, they were ready for it. Before the job opportunity even existed, they were preparing for it.

What these Levites did not know was there was going to be one of the greatest prophetic music revivals in all of history during their lifetimes, and they were going to be right in the middle of it! They didn't know the ark would be back in Israel and 24/7 worship would begin. They didn't know there was going to be a need for thousands of musicians to play in the presence of God. That had never been done before. They had no grid for what they would step into. They didn't even know they would get paid!

These Levites were going to be the ones to sing the new songs. They were the ones who first sang the songs from Psalms. Can you imagine showing up to your worship team rehearsal and King David comes in with his new song?

> *One thing I have desired of the Lord, that will I seek, that I may dwell in the house of the Lord all the days of my life, to behold the beauty of the Lord, and to inquire in His temple. (Psalm 27:4 NKJV)*

Imagine learning the melody David wrote for these lyrics and the timing of each phrase.

During the lifetime of these musicians, singers and songwriters, most of the songs in the book of Psalms were written. Think about that. The book of Psalms is filled with prophetic declarations about the glory of God, the coming Messiah, and even the end times. These songwriters were all engaging in the presence of God in the tabernacle of David and writing songs packed with new revelation.

Numerous times, the Old Testament uses the word *skill* to describe how one should play an instrument before the Lord.

> *Sing to him a new song; play **skillfully**, and shout for joy. (Psalm 33:3)*

> *Kenaniah the head Levite was in charge of the singing; that was his responsibility because he was **skillful** at it. (1 Chronicles 15:22)*

> *The Levites—all who were **skilled** in playing musical instrument. (2 Chronicles 34:12b)*

Skill cannot be replaced. Skill is not something you are born with. Skill is earned in the unseen repetition of practice. Skill grows as you surrender to discipline. Skill does not come from shortcuts or from knowing the right person. King David appointed the *skilled* Levites to serve in the musical roles. Not every Levite was skilled, and unskilled Levites were not given the musical positions.

I have seen church members ask to join a church worship team and become offended when asked to audition. They believe they have been called by God to worship (which they have), and they love the way their voice sounds when they sing in the shower. That may be all we need to be worshippers, but to be a leader in worship, skill is important. When someone doesn't pass our audition at church, we make sure to give them the feedback they need to start on the journey of growing their skills and becoming a better singer, musician, etc. We offer to connect them with voice and music teachers, and we kindly encourage them to strengthen their skill and offer to let them audition again in the future. Sadly, some do not seek to get better. I will tell you, though, that some of our great musicians and singers didn't pass an audition the first time. They had to work on a certain skill or trouble spot in their singing or musicianship. They diligently put in the effort, and now they are serving on worship teams and getting to do what they felt called by God to do.

One example of this is my husband, Caleb. Years ago, he was auditioning to sing on a worship team at IHOP–KC. Three times, he failed the vocal audition, and three times he walked away determined to grow as a singer and develop his skill. On his fourth audition, he passed! Now, he is writing songs the nations are singing and leading thousands into the presence of God through his skill as a worship leader, singer, and musician.

God anoints people to perform different roles and tasks. Skills are something we must develop. If you feel like you are supposed to be an anointed piano player, ask God to anoint you, and then go learn to play the piano! If you want to be used as a prophetic singer, ask God to anoint you, and then go learn to sing. Take some voice lessons and join a choir. Be diligent in your study of your craft.

They Were to Minister

The first thing David called the Levites to do was to minister to the Lord: *"And he appointed some of the Levites to minister before the ark of the Lord, to commemorate, to thank, and to praise the Lord God of Israel"* (1 Chron. 16:4 NKJV). It doesn't say David appointed some of the Levites to minister *before the people*. It says he appointed them to minister *before the ark of the Lord*. The ark of the Lord was the physical place on the earth where the presence of the Lord dwelt. Here, we see the primary role and function of the Levites is to minister first to the Lord before ministering to the people.

Audience of one was a Christian slogan that made its way around in the 1990s. Totally not my favorite Christianese term, but there is a picture in the term of the primary role of the Levite. Before thinking about the crowds of people or the people in your church who need to be led into worship, minister to the Lord. We worship God because He is worthy and deserving, but also because He desires our worship. Your *singing to God* is what ministers to His heart, not necessarily your *singing about Him* in front of people.

It is too easy to become lost in the work of the ministry. We see the needs of the people, and we do our very, very best to minister and meet those needs. Now, let me be clear. There is nothing wrong with that. But if we do all those things and see them as our only ministry, then we miss out on the most important thing—the one thing of Psalm 27:4.

Our primary focus, our one thing, our first ministry—not only as leaders in music ministry but as human beings—is to minister to the heart of God, to be in His presence and gaze on His beauty, to communicate and dialogue (pray), and to worship Him and love Him with the very core of our beings. Everything else will and should flow from this place. Seek first His Kingdom. Then all these other things are added. This biblical principle from Matthew 6:33 extends to worship. Worship lead first as your ministry to Jesus. Then leading the people will follow.

They Were to Commemorate

The next thing David told the Levites to do in 1 Chronicles 16:4 was to commemorate the Lord God. To commemorate means to recall or to show respect. Throughout Old Testament history, we see the people of Israel commemorating the mighty acts of the Lord on their behalf. One way remembering or commemorating was instilled in their culture was through their retelling the stories of their forefathers. So much of their culture and history was preserved through the art of oral tradition. The retelling of the ways God saved them was part of the Levitical role.

The old hymn, "I Surrender All," has a lyric in the second verse that highlights this idea. "Here I raise my Ebenezer, hither by thy help I come. And I hope by thy good pleasure safely to arrive at home." This lyric was inspired by 1 Samuel 7:12 where Samuel took a stone, named it Ebenezer, and said, "Thus far the Lord has helped us."

The word or name *Ebenezer* means stone of help. When God would move on behalf of Israel, the people of God would build an altar made of stones to the Lord right there as an act of worship and remembrance for what He did. They would construct the altar to be tall enough so as to be visible from far away. They would build the altar, make a sacrifice, worship, then continue their journey. As they faced more hardship along the way, they could physically look back to the altars they had built and maybe still see the smoke rising in the distance and remember how the Lord had come through for them in the past. This would give them courage and faith that God would move again to save and deliver in their present as well as in their future.

I know we no longer build physical altars, but when we celebrate the breakthrough of a trial, we worship and exalt Jesus. We build an altar of remembrance in our hearts. These altars are spread throughout our walks with God. The altars are the remembrance of the testimony of Jesus in our lives. We look back to these altars when we are faced with new difficulties. We look ahead to the coming breakthrough as we also look back to the Ebenezers we have raised after every victory. We can say we have never seen the righteous forsaken as we look back upon the altars that commemorate our God and His perfect leadership in our lives.

In worship, we can worship God simply for who He is. He is enough. But we can also worship Him for what He has done. Many of my own personal prophetic songs have been encouraging the room to remember; to remember who He is and what He has done. You don't want only to remember what He has done for others or the stories of breakthroughs in the Bible or in a friend's life. You also want to remember the deeply personal way Jesus has shown Himself faithful time and time again in your own crisis and in your own times of need, and you want to remember those personal times for your own edification and encouragement.

They Were to Thank

Next, in 1 Chronicles 16:4, David told the Levites to thank the Lord. Psalm 100 is one of my favorite psalms to read aloud during the call to worship at our weekend services because it's a call to give thanks to God. As we enter into worship, I love exhorting the room with this psalm:

> *Make a joyful shout to the Lord, all you lands! Serve the Lord with gladness; come before His presence with singing. Know that the Lord, He is God; it is He who has made us, and not we ourselves; we are His people and the sheep of His pasture.* **Enter into His gates with thanksgiving, and into His courts with praise. Be thankful to Him, and bless His name.** *For the Lord is good; His mercy is everlasting, and His truth endures to all generations.*

What does it mean to "enter into His gates with thanksgiving"? First, I see those "enter here" signs in my head. It's like the flashing signs that say, "Entrance this way!" This is where we start. A gate is like a door. It is the way in. These verses instruct us how to come into and be in His presence. Walk through the gate of thanksgiving. This isn't a rule or a law; it's wisdom. Thankfulness can turn our moods from selfish loathing to gratefulness and contentment.

I spent a few months contributing to a thankfulness journal. Every day, I would write a few things for which I was thankful. I would write my thankfulness for the breeze on a summer day or the way my three-year-old leaned in for a big kiss after he woke up from a nap. The big things and the little moments found their way into my journal. During this time, I found myself having a much more positive and content outlook on my life. I was able to slow down and see with a new lens, a lens of gratitude and thankfulness.

When we express thankfulness and gratitude to God, it blesses Him; but more than that, it does something supernatural in our souls. As we open our mouths and express sincere thanks to God for who He is or what He has done, we are opening the gate and entering His presence. Thankfulness then opens the door to the courts of praise.

They Were to Praise

The last charge that David gave the Levites in 1 Chronicles 16:4 was to praise the Lord God of Israel. As a worshipper, you should know all about praise. It's the expression of adoration from our hearts that is declared to others and to the One we are adoring.

By definition, praise cannot be hidden. It's not something we do in secret or quietly so we cannot be heard. If we want to praise a person for an accolade, we do it loudly so they can hear us. Or we praise them in front of a crowd so their accomplishment can be known to everyone.

Praise is so simple we can forget to do it. Words of affirmation are not my husband's love language. I use this as an excuse sometimes and just don't tell him as much as I should that he's awesome. Just the other day, on his day off, he tackled an insane to-do list. Many of the things on his list were small house projects I had been nagging him about for the last five months. I was out of the house most of that day, and when I got home, I immediately noticed he had fixed two of the doors that hadn't been working properly for some time. And I am embarrassed to admit it, but I didn't really say anything. I just shrugged off his fixing the doors as simply part of his role as a member of our family. I wasn't even going to acknowledge his hard work and sacrifice on his day off. Not cool, I know. Thankfully, Caleb called me out, and I quickly realized he needed some affirmation (praise). I told him how thankful I was that he fixed the doors and what a hero he was for knocking out his whole to-do-list that day.

God doesn't need our praise, but He absolutely deserves it. And we *need* to offer praise. We get unhealthy when we don't recognize what He has done. We get unhealthy when we take God for granted.

Praise is so simple we forget the power of it. We need to remind ourselves that God inhabits our praise. He shows up in power when we praise Him. It's in our praise that He rides in and is glorified.

The word *praise* in 1 Chronicles 16:4 is the Hebrew word *hallal*. Did you know there are seven different Hebrew words for our English word *praise*? Here they are:

1. *Halal* is the root word for praise. It's where we get the derivative *hallelujah*, which is a word that will never need to be translated into another language because it's a word that transcends language. It is the same in every single language. (Example: Ps. 150:1)
2. *Yadah* is a verb that means to extend or lift the hand. This posture of our bodies is praise. We know our hearts are postured to praise, but here is a way we praise with our bodies. Praise is meant to be something our body, soul, and spirit can all engage in at the same time. (Example: Ps. 107:15)
3. *Towdah* is an extension of the hand in adoration, thanking God for things not yet received. This is another way we praise body, soul, and spirit. And it is praise with faith, believing and thanking God for what you do not have yet or what He has yet to do. (Example: Ps. 50:14)
4. *Shabach* means to shout. (Example: Ps. 145:4)
5. *Barach* is to kneel down or salute, to bless. (Example: Ps. 34:1)
6. *Zamar* means to play an instrument or sing. (Example: Ps. 21:13)
7. *Tehillah* is another word that means to sing. (Example: Ps. 22:3)

Modern-Day Levites

Today in church, worship leaders, singers, and musicians are modern-day Levites. We no longer need priests to sacrifice live animals for the atonement for sin, guilt offerings, burnt offerings, or fellowship offerings. In every way, Jesus the Lamb of God was the final and only sacrifice that satisfied the wrath of God against our sin. Therefore, the sacrificial system and many of the roles of the priest are no longer needed.

However, the roles that Levites fulfilled in the tabernacle of David—such as worship leader, singer, and musician—are needed now, maybe more than ever. Many young and old are feeling stirred and called to be established in the house of God, ministering to the heart of God. God is setting apart ones to be consecrated and purified. Malachi 3:3 is a verse for us in this day. God is purifying the Levites. He is consecrating and setting apart a generation of worshippers, ones who will offer to the Lord a sacrifice and an offering worth receiving. Oh, that we would be Levites in the house of God who are so connected to the heart of God that it is our joy and delight to offer our worship and it is our great honor to lead others in doing the same.

> **God is purifying the Levites. He is consecrating and setting apart a generation of worshippers, ones who will offer to the Lord a sacrifice and an offering worth receiving. Oh, that we would be Levites in the house of God who are so connected to the heart of God that it is our joy and delight to offer our worship and it is our great honor to lead others in doing the same.**

Closing Prayer

Pray this prayer with me. It may help to read it aloud.

Father,
Thank You that in this day You are raising up Levites across the globe to be worshippers in Your house. I agree with Your heart and ask that You would raise them up. Call us out of insecurity and into our identity as priests and

Levites before You. Would You purify our hearts and set us apart for such a time as this? Help us find our hope and strength in You. You are our inheritance and our cup. Thank You for the lots that have fallen for us in pleasant places.

We take this opportunity right now to praise You. We praise You for Your sovereignty, the way You hold the world and our hearts together. We give You all of our praise and adoration. We put it all on You. We step into our role as a Levite and say yes *to ministering first to Your heart. We will lead ourselves and then others into commemorating all You are and all You have done. We will thank You and praise You with all that we are and lead Your people to do the same.*

Thank You for this high calling.
Amen.

Prompt

When did you first recognize your call to worship?

A Testimony

I was going through a pretty hard time. I was battling lots of discouragement in my career, disappointment related to some circumstances affecting my loved ones, and some depression. Life felt like it was spiraling out of control.

On the weekend, my husband and I went to church, and I just remember the worship leader got up there and said he was going to sing a little something that God had spoken to him the night before. And though it wasn't completely spontaneous, I felt like every word was straight from God to me: "I never abandoned or left you alone. I didn't fall asleep. I didn't fall off My throne. I'm still holding on to the stars in My hands. I am still walking among the lampstands. Death doesn't scare Me. I conquered the grave. The storm might be coming, but I walk on waves. . . . It's My turn now."

And it completely broke me. I felt that this prophetic word was for our church and for me as an individual. The Holy Spirit convicted me instantly of His sovereignty. All my circumstances were not under my control, nor did they have to be. God was telling me through the prophetic song that He was in control of everything and that He was far greater than anything I was facing. I was able to extend my hands and give all my distress up to God. The peace that followed allowed me to approach everything I was going through with a different perspective. It allowed me to speak into the lives of others who were also being burdened by the same circumstances. And it was an instant reminder that God will fight for me. I only needed to be still and give Him my praise.

—Lindsey

Prophetic Songs in the Bible

In this chapter, I want to take you through some of the songs in the Bible. There are at least 185 songs in the Scriptures. There are songs of praise, songs of lament, songs for battle, and songs with prophetic declarations. Psalms, Song of Solomon, and Lamentations are all songbooks with the entirety of their contents being songs. This will not be an exhaustive overview but merely a quick look at only a few of the powerful songs written and sung in the Bible.

As we seek to understand the role of the new song and prophetic singers in our day, it is important to see throughout biblical history the way these songs were used by God to lead individuals, families, armies, and nations. Their prophetic declarations captured in the Word of God give us insight into what contexts prophetic songs were sung and the way they shaped history and prophesied change, administered encouragement, and brought to remembrance the greatness of God.

The Song of Moses

The Song of Moses is the first song recorded in the Bible. This song was sung immediately following the deliverance of God's people from the hands of the Egyptians. It appears in Exodus 15:1–3.

> *"I will sing to the Lord, For He has triumphed gloriously! The horse and its rider He has thrown into the sea! The Lord is my strength and song, And He has become my salvation; He is my God, and I will praise Him; My father's God, and I will exalt Him." (NKJV)*

Israel had been enslaved for 400 years. Generation after generation cried out for God to deliver them from slavery and lead them into the Promised Land that He pledged to their forefathers—Abraham, Isaac, and Jacob. God raised up Moses to deliver the people, and after the ten plagues culminated with the killing of the firstborn, Pharoah released the people.

A little time passed before Pharoah realized what this decision would mean for himself and his nation. He changed his mind and sent the strength of his army in pursuit of the Israelites. Israel became trapped between the Egyptian army and the Red Sea. God miraculously split the sea in another act of deliverance, and the people of God crossed on dry land while the Egyptian chariots drowned in the middle of the sea.

A New Thing, A New Song

When God does a new thing, the people of God sing a new song. The songs Israel sang during the generations of captivity were not the songs to sing after their great moment of deliverance from the Egyptians. They needed a new song to sing. They needed a song to fully express the greatness of their God and celebrate their deliverance. And this is how the song of Moses begins, and the song continues for a total of eighteen verses, declaring the greatness of God and retelling His mighty works.

The Israelites sang of what they just had experienced. They sang of their deliverance by the hand of God. Immediately, they chose to remember and celebrate what God had done for them. They sang of God's triumph over Pharoah. They sang to praise, and they sang to remember directly following the miracle of their deliverance from Egypt and the parting of the Red Sea. Then at the end of the song, in the last two verses, they began to prophesy what God would do next:

> **When God does a new thing, the people of God sing a new song.**

You will bring them and plant them in the mountain of Your inheritance, the place, O Lord, which You have made for Your dwelling, the sanctuary, O Lord, which Your hands have established. The Lord shall reign forever and ever. (Exodus 15:17–18 NASB1995)

The people of God prophesied their own destiny. They prophesied they would make it to the land God promised their forefathers. They prophesied Israel would be planted in the Promised Land and in the mountain of God when Jesus returns and rules and reigns on the earth as King.

The Power of Every Voice

The best singer did not stand up in this moment and sing a solo for everyone to hear. This song was not a solo that Moses sang to the people. Moses led the sons of Israel to sing it with him. Every man joined in the song. Every man opened his mouth and with his own voice sang the new song. It doesn't say the gifted sang the new song. It doesn't even say the ones who were closest to Moses sang. It says *all* the men. This was wide-scale participation. This was 100 percent agreement and engagement with the new song. This was corporate worship.

God is moved by such a display of worship, and every man who sings and participates in this kind of singing has his heart aligned with what God is doing and saying on the earth.

In the singing of the Israelites, we see unity among them as they sang their song together.

The song of Moses tells us three things about prophetic songs and how they can be used today:

1. The new song encourages us to remember the new thing God is doing, and in this case, it was the deliverance of His people!
2. The new song is full of praise.
3. The new song is for *every voice* to sing. The new song is not just for the leaders or the gifted few to sing. It is for everyone.

The Song of Miriam

In the same chapter where the Song of Moses appears, we find the Song of Miriam. We read:

> *Then Miriam the prophet, Aaron's sister, took a timbrel in her hand, and all the women followed her, with timbrels and dancing. Miriam sang to them: "Sing to the Lord, for he is highly exalted. Both horse and driver he has hurled into the sea.""* Exodus 15:20–21

This song is recorded in Exodus directly following the Song of Moses, and it may be safe to assume it occurred right after Moses' song.

First, you will notice right away that Miriam's song is a repeat of the first two lines of Moses' song. Moses and the men began their song with strong and powerful lines that were worth repeating, but they had more content to get through in their song as the verses of the song contained details, examples, and stories. The first two lines encompassed the two main ideas of the entire song. The first idea was to sing praise to the Lord, and the second idea was why they were to sing praise.

Once the men had finished their song, Miriam led the women in the first recorded prophetic chorus! She chose the two lines that best captured the heart and intent of Moses' song, and she sang them out again. I can just see Miriam listening to the Song of Moses and eyeing her timbrel only a few feet away from her. Maybe the melody of the first two lines stuck with her, and she felt the life that was on them. She brought back the main idea of Moses' song. As the women joined in and the chorus rang out throughout the camp, I have to assume they kept singing it over and over again. Miriam had her timbrel, and I have to guess there were other instruments being played, too. I bet the celebration that took place as the women joined in with Miriam was a sight and sound to behold. The entire camp was singing and rejoicing as they celebrated and praised God for setting them free.

The new song brought joy!

All the women could join in with the simple chorus that encompassed the song, and it unified the people. The chorus was easy to learn, simple enough to sing, and it facilitated corporate, unified, and joyful worship.

We use choruses all the time to bring home the main idea of a prayer or a prophetic declaration. Even in our worship songs, the chorus is typically the part of the song that is repeated the most because it carries the main message of the song. The chorus is usually the catchiest part of the song, and it tends to stick with you even if you forget the verses.

To say it all again, choruses typically are easy to learn, simple to sing, and contain the main idea of the song. So, next time you hear an awesome chorus, you can thank the prophetess Miriam for giving us the first chorus ever recorded in biblical history.

Not only was Miriam's song a chorus, but it was also the first example we have of responsive singing. Another term for responsive singing is antiphonal singing. The word *antiphonal* comes from the root word *antiphon*. *Merriam-Webster's Dictionary* states the meaning of *antiphon* as "a psalm, anthem, or verse sung responsively" or "a verse usually from Scripture said or sung before and after a canticle, psalm, or psalm verse as part of the liturgy." Miriam responded to the original song Moses and the men sang. This back-and-forth singing is seen throughout church history. Antiphonal singing has been part of church history since Miriam sang her chorus. We also see it in Gregorian chants, call-and-response liturgy, and modern worship.

Back in the 90s, we had loads of worship songs that included this idea of responsive singing. Songs like, "I will Give You All My Worship," "Light the Fire in My Heart," "Shout to the North," and many others had the men sing one line or part of the song and the women sing a different part. Since then, we have seen antiphonal singing become part of the worldwide worship and prayer movement championed by the IHOP–KC and replicated by houses of prayer across the world and referenced by churches, small groups, and other prayer gatherings. This form of antiphonal singing looks like a handful of singers, one by one, singing supporting phrases during a prayer meeting or worship context.

The Shortest Song

You have heard this short song before. Let me set the stage for when it first debuted. For years, the ark of the covenant was hosted by David's tabernacle in Jerusalem. David pitched a tent and commanded the Levites to lead 24/7 prayer and worship in the presence of God. It was in David's heart to build a permanent house for the presence of the Lord to dwell. First Chronicles 17:1–2 says, *"Now it came to pass, when David was dwelling in his house, that David said to Nathan the prophet, 'See now, I dwell in a house of cedar, but the ark of the covenant of the Lord is under tent curtains'"* (NKJV).

The author of Psalm 132 remembered David's vow to the Lord in verses 3–4,

> *Surely I will not go into the chamber of my house, or go up to the comfort of my bed; I will not give sleep to my eyes or slumber to my eyelids, until I find a place for the Lord, a dwelling place for the Mighty One of Jacob. (NKJV)*

Years went by, and ultimately, David's son Solomon was the one who built the temple for the Lord. The shortest song in the Bible was sung as the singers, musicians, and all the Levites along with the elders and all the men of Israel gathered to bring the ark of the covenant and the other tabernacle furnishings to the temple. Second Chronicles 5:13–14 tells us,

> *Indeed it came to pass, when the trumpeters and singers were as one, to make one sound to be heard in praising and*

*thanking the Lord, and when they lifted up their voice with the trumpets and cymbals and instruments of music, and praised the Lord, saying: "For He is good, **for His mercy endures forever,**" that the house, the house of the Lord, was filled with a cloud, so that the priests could not continue ministering because of the cloud; for the glory of the Lord filled the house of God. (NKJV)*

King Solomon gave a grand speech to open the temple, said a prayer of dedication, and at the end of his prayer he invited the Lord to arise to His resting place. Second Chronicles 7:1–3 reads,

*When Solomon had finished praying, fire came down from heaven and consumed the burnt offering and the sacrifices; and the glory of the Lord filled the temple. And the priests could not enter the house of the Lord, because the glory of the Lord had filled the Lord's house. When all the children of Israel saw how the fire came down, and the glory of the Lord on the temple, they bowed their faces to the ground on the pavement, and worshipped and praised the Lord, saying: "For He is good, **for His mercy endures forever.**" (NKJV)*

They closed the dedication of the temple with the simple, yet profound song that they opened with, and again the glory of God filled the temple.

Oftentimes, when I am trying to write a song, I get lost in long, flowery language that I would never actually say in a conversation, but somehow I think my song needs to be full of poetry, rhyme, and word tricks. I have too many examples to count of instances where I tried to have the coolest anthem and tried too hard to create a spontaneous chorus that was so good it would spark the return of Jesus! I remember trying to create spur of the moment metaphors, creative similes, rhythms, rhymes, etc. I ended up taking three verses to get down to the point of what I was trying to say. My chorus wasn't corporate because no one could sing it with me. *Too many words or too many ideas and themes crammed into a chorus will overcomplicate what should be simple.* The song in 2 Chronicles shows us that sometimes less is more. Two lines were anointed, and simple praise ushered in the presence of God to rest in a space.

Sometimes, we can get hung up on creating something new and profound. There can be this pressure to come up with the next best thing. Creating choruses spontaneously is not always the best place to feel that pressure. I constantly coach our singers that it is not about the best, new way to say something or the most creative phrase. If a phrase is powerful and contains the message required for the moment, use it! The simple phrase in 2 Chronicles 5, *"for His love endures forever,"* was sung again in Psalm 136. In fact, Psalm 136 repeats this chorus 26 times! And the repetition itself makes a powerful statement.

The first nine verses of Psalm 136 praise God for who He is and, more specifically, who He is as the Creator. Verses 10 through 22 praise Him for all that He has done for the people of God. This was an overview of the personal testimony the Israelites had with God and the mighty acts God did to save and rescue them time and time again. Verses 23 and 24 are ways now in the present that God is faithful. The song ends in verse 25 like the way it began: *"Give thanks to the God of heaven. His love endures forever!"*

Slowly read through Psalm 136. Take in the progression and beauty of this song. See the statement after each statement of praise.

> *Give thanks to the Lord, for he is good. His love endures forever. Give thanks to the God of gods. His love endures forever. Give thanks to the Lord of lords: His love endures forever: to him who alone does great wonders, His love endures forever: who by his understanding made the heavens, His love endures forever: who spread out the earth upon the waters, His love endures forever: who made the great lights—His love endures forever: the sun to govern the day, His love endures forever: the moon and starts to govern the night; His love endures forever: to him who struck down the firstborn of Egypt His love endures forever: and brought Israel out from among them His love endures forever: with a might hand and outstretched arm; His love*

endures forever: to him who struck down great kings, His love endures forever: and killed mighty kings—His love endures forever: and Og king of Bashan—His love endures forever: and gave their land as an inheritance, His love endures forever: an inheritance to his servant Israel. His love endures forever. He remembered us in our low estate His love endures forever: and freed us from our enemies. His love endures forever. He gives food to every creature. His love endures forever. Give thanks to the God of heaven. His love endures forever.

Notice your own spirit begin to be filled with thankfulness and gratitude. Statements of praise and remembrance have the power to fill us with hope and faith.

We see this exact song sung yet again in Israel's history about 100 years later in 2 Chronicles 20. Judah was being threatened by the Moabites and Ammonites. King Jehoshaphat called a nationwide fast to pray to the Lord for help. In the middle of the fast, a Levite, a descendant of Asaph, the chief prophetic musician from King David's day, stood up and declared the word of the Lord. He said that they would not have to fight in the battle but should position themselves to see the salvation of the Lord.

Jehoshaphat and the people heard the word of the Lord, and they responded in worship. The very next day, they went out to meet the enemy armies. Jehoshaphat appointed some of the people to sing and praise the Lord as they went out to battle, and this was the song they chose:

"Give thanks to the Lord, for His love endures forever." 2 Chronicles 20:21b

This chorus was now over 100 years old. Yet it was the simple song of praise the appointed singers felt led prophetically to sing and declare as they led the way into battle.

Next, we see the God of the breakthrough cause the enemy armies to attack one another as the worshippers worshipped. By the time the people of God arrived at the battle scene, the entire enemy armies had been annihilated by each other! Praise was the way they could participate in the breakthrough that was coming. This is how we are to fight the battles we face. We are to lead in praise. This battle scene gives us a perfect picture of how we are to position ourselves when we face adversity—our eyes looking at Jesus and our hearts declaring the greatness of God and our lips praising Him for who He is.

This is not the only instance when God commanded the singers and worshippers to lead the charge into battle. In Joshua 6, we see the trumpet blast and a mighty shout from the people was the praise the Lord was looking for. When the people of God praised, the walls of Jericho came crashing down. Praise brings faith, and praise is linked to breakthrough!

The shortest song in the Bible shows us:

1. Length does not speak to the power or anointing of the new song.
2. Choruses unify people to sing the new song together.
3. Bringing back old, anointed choruses that worked in the past is a form of singing the new song.

Songs from the Book of Revelation

The book of Revelation has over a dozen songs more commonly known as the Hymns of Revelation. These hymns are short but filled with truth and declare who God is, who Jesus is, and the worthiness of Jesus. These songs came straight from the throne room of heaven, and John saw and heard these singing moments in heaven and was able to transcribe the songs sung there. These declarations of truth have been rewritten into many of our worship songs. I will end this chapter with a few of these hymns. As you read them, see them with fresh eyes. These songs are gifts to us from heaven.

> *"Holy, holy, holy is the Lord God Almighty,' who was, and is, and is to come." (Revelation 4:8)*

"You are worthy, our Lord and God, to receive glory and honor and power, for you created all things, and by your will they were created and have their being." (Revelation 4:11)

"You are worthy to take the scroll and to open its seals, because you were slain, and with your blood you purchased for God persons from every tribe and language and people and nation. You have made them to be a kingdom and priests to serve our God, and they will reign on the earth." (Revelation 5:9–10)

"Worthy is the Lamb, who was slain, to receive power and wealth and wisdom and strength and honor and glory and praise!" (Revelation 5:12)

"To him who sits on the throne and to the Lamb be praise and honor and glory and power, for ever and ever!" (Revelation 5:13)

Closing Prayer

Pray this prayer with me over yourself. It may help to read it aloud.

Father,
Thank You for the songs scattered throughout Scripture. Thank You for the melodies accompanying each song that we have not yet heard. I ask that the prophetic songs would arise in Your church, that our hearts would be awakened to the power of the new song.
　Holy Spirit, would You release revelation to Your songbirds. Just as John received so many hymns sung around the throne room of heaven, would You release prophetic utterances to Your sons and Your daughters? I pray for mighty choruses to be released, songs of remembrance, songs that tell stories of Your greatness. I ask that a wave of sound would bring revelation to the Church and that we would sing sound theology with hearts that have encountered Your Spirit. I truly believe there is another wave coming; it's a wave of

prophetic voices and a wave of prophetic utterances coming through song. Would You do it, and would You release the new song?
    Amen.

Prompt

Journal your own rendition of the Song of Moses.

Reflect on your own story. What are some of the things the Lord has brought you out of and delivered you from?

Journal a "new song" like Moses and Miriam sang. No pressure to write a complete song or to make it poetic. Just express what wells up in your heart when you think of the mercy and kindness of the Lord to bring you out of darkness and into His glorious light. Remember His faithfulness to deliver you and keep you through every trial and circumstance. Write from this place.

A Testimony

I grew up as a pastor's kid in Ohio. I was super involved in church and always concerned with saying and doing the right thing, knowing that what I did would reflect on the church and my parents. I also put that pressure on myself in my walk with the Lord. I felt like I was always striving to do and say the right thing to gain His love and approval. I felt like I didn't read my Bible enough or didn't talk about God enough with friends at school. I felt like God was always disappointed in me.

About twelve years ago, when I was in my third year of ministry school, during one of our prayer times, I heard the prophetic song, "Do you know the way you move Me." As it began to play, I felt like it was the Father singing straight to me, "I see every time you look at Me. I'm not disappointed in you. I love you, thank you." I began to weep as twenty years of what I had known about God's love was completely transformed. I have honestly felt free since that day. It was a deep revelation of the kindness of the Father.

I believe so strongly in prophetic worship because of the impact it has made in my life, and I've seen it impact others over and over again as well.

—Allison

Hearing the Voice of God

God still speaks! This is the required groundwork we must lay before we dive into a chapter about hearing God's voice. We must believe that He speaks! We serve a God who loves to speak. Not that He spoke, or used to speak, then decided to be distant. We believe He is still speaking today!

Secondly, He is speaking to us, His Church. Our God is not silent. He has something to say. He has wisdom, counsel, hope, truth, love, and so much more to communicate to us corporately.

Thirdly, God is speaking to *you*. It can be harder to believe when we make it personal. "Of course God speaks. Yes, I believe that, and sure, I believe He is speaking to the Church, but God is speaking to me? I'm not so sure about that." You may struggle with knowing how to hear His voice or how to distinguish His voice from all the other voices you hear. And then there is always the possibility you struggle with believing He would want to speak to you. Let me assure you He is intimately involved in your life and wants you to hear what is on His heart. He wants you as His sheep to know His voice. This chapter is filled with tools to help you on your journey of hearing God.

For this chapter, I have the great honor to introduce you to my dear friend Anna Asbury. Anna has been walking out the calling of prophetic singer for decades with grace and anointing. You are probably already familiar with her ministry and have been touched by her leadership in worship and the prophetic. She hears the voice of God and has such a gift for releasing it to the Body of Christ. She has been practicing hearing the voice of God for decades, and I can't wait for you to receive from her wisdom. She was gracious enough to beautifully pen this chapter on hearing God's voice.

Beginnings

I remember it like it was yesterday. The first time I was a part of prophetic worship, I was in awe. I could not get enough. I wanted to be a part of all the prophetic worship times I could get myself in. The presence of God was very present, and the words the singers sang seemed to be reading my mail. It was a new deeper way of encountering God through music and song, and I was hooked. Honestly, I still am to this day. In fact, this very day Cory and I were having another conversation about prophetic worship, and how it's the real, raw, unrehearsed moments that we still crave. The space where we ask and allow the Holy Spirit to come and have His way.

Space, rest, letting go of control, and playing in the background are all things I think of when I think about presence-based worship. When God shows up in a set, and the musicians and singers engage in what He's up to and what He's saying, well, there's just nothing quite like it. You could say I'm addicted to His presence, His voice, His words—all of it. Isn't that what it's all about? Why would I ever want to do a moment of worship without Him leading us?

Of course we prepare, and we bring the songs, and we have the backbone of the set ready to go. But it would be so sorrowful if one day we showed up to our sets, sang our songs, finished, and never once heard what God was singing, never once asked Him what He was speaking, and never once took the backseat for a moment to let Him lead the room while we followed. This is what this chapter is about. I desire to give you the tools to get you to a place where you can hear the Father's voice, know who you are as a daughter or son, and sing from that position in any moment or in any place. This gift of prophecy isn't just for the gifted, special ones. You have a voice. With the right tools, you can be a prophetic singer.

Hearing His Voice

John 1:1 tells us that Jesus is the very Word of God. The *Logos* is God active in creation, revelation, and redemption. Jesus Christ not only gives God's Word to us humans, but He is the Word. The *Logos* is God, begotten and therefore distinguishable from the Father, but being God, He is of the same substance (essence). If He bears the very name, *The Word*, then it would be right to assume that He does indeed speak.

From the beginning He has been speaking, and He has never stopped. It was His very voice that put the planets in flight and hung the stars in their places. It was His very voice that illuminated the sky with hues of blue. It was His voice that spoke and created life. Animals, birds, fish, and the culmination of it all, humans, were His very voice and His breath that formed our beings from dust. Power and beauty are the makeup and essence of The Word. When we look at our world, creation, and take in what God has declared into existence, does it not fill you with wonder and anticipation to hear and discover more? So that leads us to the looming question, how do we undam the roaring waterfall of His voice to become a constant flowing river in our lives?

> You could say I'm addicted to His presence, His voice, His words—all of it. Isn't that what it's all about? Why would I ever want to do a moment of worship without Him leading us?

Through my years of asking and searching there have been a few tools I daily come back to, to aid me in my pursuit of His voice. You won't find a formula or singular method in these pages. Those have never worked with my other relationships either. We must approach hearing His voice as relational, not scientific.

Journaling

When I was thirteen years old, I attended my first creative worship camp in the hills of North Carolina. It was there that I met now lifelong friends Jonathan and Melissa Helser. You probably know them for some of their anthems, "No Longer Slaves," "I Raise a Hallelujah," and "Abba, I belong to You." Their songs are like the beautiful branches of a healthy tree, the evidence of a strong root system deep in the ground. Songs of truth are birthed in the place of relationship, and relationship requires conversation between two people. The Helsers had something I wanted, a deep friendship and sonship with God. I was provoked with jealousy to know the secrets of how they reached this place. It was at their camp that I discovered one of the most important tools to this date on how to hear the voice of God in my life.

I'm sure you are familiar with journaling. Maybe you think of it as a diary, a place to write your thoughts, record your day, and get a little space to process things through writing. The thought of journaling is not a new concept; however, what I began to learn through the Helsers was that writing down my inward most sincere prayers before God, and then writing down His voice and thoughts back to me would absolutely change my life. Essentially, it's what we read repeatedly in the Psalms. David wrote His most sincere and, at times, rather dramatic prayers and songs to God. You may be thinking, *What? How in the world do you hear God's voice and write down what He says? What if I hear wrong? What if it's negative and puts me in a deeper hole than I was in when I started?*

Journaling in sincerity and honesty does take time to get used to, but it also takes time to get to know someone. Think of journaling as a safe space to start to have real conversation with your Creator, Friend, Savior, and Redeemer. This is the place that you tell Him everything: your hopes, dreams, fears, your deepest thoughts. This is also the place where you give Him the space to respond. It may start out as just a word or a few words. It may be a scripture that comes to mind or even a picture that you want to draw. The creativity in this process is endless. There is no set rule of how to do it completely right. The purpose is simply to talk and build relationship. Hear the tender love and affection of the Father speaking over you. I can also guarantee you that if it's a negative thing you hear, you should stop and ask again. He is slow to anger and rich in love. Like He spoke to Elijah in the cave, He usually comes in a whisper rather than a loud, resounding trumpet of a voice.

So, grab a journal, one that you love! It needs to be something that inspires you, whether you love leather or want to make a mod podge of a journal from your favorite magazine clippings, or you love bright colors with words. Whatever it is, grab one that screams you. Then sit down and take some time to ask the Holy Spirit to help you open your heart and release the deep things inside. Write the date and place you are at so you can come back and remember when you want to. Then start writing out your heart before the Lord.

When you have finished, take a moment and ask the Holy Spirit to reveal to you the heart of the Father. Ask and you shall receive, knock and the door will open. Again, don't be discouraged if you don't hear very much the first time you ask. Hearing God's voice is like a muscle. The more you work it, the easier it is to hear Him, and you recognize His voice much more. It takes time to tune your ear to hear Him. At the end of this chapter, there will be space to practice. This is something I try and do daily. It has been the anchor for me in tuning my ears to hear what God is speaking, instead of what the world may be saying. It is such an important tool for developing a relationship with God.

Reading and Singing the Scripture

In Matthew 4:4, Jesus said, *"It is written: 'Man shall not live on bread alone, but on every word that comes from the mouth of God.'"* As I spoke about in the beginning of this chapter, God is always speaking, and the best place to hear His voice is through His Word.

Hebrews 4:12 says,

> *For the word of God is living and active, sharper than any two-edged sword, piercing to the division of soul and of spirit, of joints and of marrow, and discerning the thoughts and intentions of the heart. (ESV)*

If we are to take the Word for what it says, and if this verse is true, then when I sit down in the morning to read the Scriptures, this should be the best part of my day! Something that I've learned over the years is that I cannot base what is happening in my spirit on my emotions or feelings. There are some days when I read the Scriptures and feel nothing, absolutely nothing. However, I know because of Hebrews 4:12 that there is something greater working and moving as I humble myself and lean in for instruction through the Word. The Holy Spirit takes the living, active, alive words of the Scripture and applies them to my heart to disciple and train me. He uses the words to form my inner being, giving me strength, love, and life (see Eph. 3:17–19).

Psalm 119:105 says, *"Your word is a lamp for my feet, a light on my path."* The Scripture literally changes lives. It comes in and brings light to our hearts. It brings wisdom to situations we may not have answers for. It brings truth where we are believing lies. The Scripture is God's voice to us, the love letter of His heart, guiding and leading us through our days. The Scriptures are the Word of God. I encourage you, if you are wavering in your belief of the power of the Word, to do a google search of "Word of God scriptures." I bet you'll be blown away with all the scriptures that pop up, and I bet you'll get excited about reading the Word becoming a discipline in your life, especially after reading about all the ways the Word empowers your life.

Here is how I got started hearing God's voice through reading, singing and praying the Scriptures. When I was eighteen, I left home to attend an internship for six months at IHOP–KC. IHOP is a ministry like the tabernacle of David. It has been going 24/7 with worship and prayer since 1999. The heart of the mission's base is night-and-day prayer with worship. Two figures from the Bible who it is inspired by are Anna, one of the first evangelists and intercessors in the New Testament, who prayed and fasted for over sixty years before Jesus' first coming, and King David, who organized

> **Today, when I sing, speak, journal, or use whatever other avenue to connect with God, I can hear those scriptures come up in my heart, and I know the sound of His voice. It sounds like His Word.**

and paid 4,000 musicians and 288 singers to worship God night and day (see Luke 2:37; 1 Chron. 23:1–25:31). What began as a six-month internship became nine years of praying, singing, and studying the Word of God. Just like Anna and David, I felt this deep calling to minister before the Lord for the rest of my life. Going in, I would have never known that I would or that I could even spend that many years, months, days, and hours doing the same thing, but the invitation to be a Levite before the Lord was a glorious and beautiful thing. In fact, I thought Cory and I would be there forever. Why do I bring this up now while I'm writing about hearing the voice of God through reading the Scripture?

> **Every time you open the Word of God, He's there waiting to reveal something new and living to your heart.**

Well, I can tell you that—after set after set of singing, reading, and praying the Scripture—I became what I like to refer to as a singing seminary. We would spend months and months as a team, day after day, in one passage and get absolutely captivated with the new life and the new thing God was speaking to us every single time. Now, don't get me wrong. There were bad sets and hard days where we felt nothing and didn't want to be there. However, what we did still counted, and the seed of God's Word was still planted. The Word of God that is living and active began to take root deeply in my life.

Today, when I sing, speak, journal, or use whatever other avenue to connect with God, I can hear those scriptures come up in my heart, and I know the sound of His voice. It sounds like His Word. Even today as I was journaling out His voice over me, it started with Him speaking a scripture over me, reminding me of who He is and who I am. Every time you open the Word of God, He's there waiting to reveal something new and living to your heart. He's ready to breathe life and truth deep inside you. If you put into practice the reading and studying of the Word of God, you will begin to know His gracious tone and confidently know His delight and intentions for your life. The Scripture speaks, and all it takes is a moment of listening to hear it.

Hearing through Creation

Playing outside was a major part of my childhood. I remember spending countless hours in the woods. I would pretend that I was lost and needed to be rescued, or that I was a mother taking care of many orphaned children, or that I was a princess hiding from a wicked stepmother deep in the woods. Cornfields were enticing mazes waiting to be conquered, and rivers were the waters waiting to carry me to my next adventure.

Where I grew up in Eastern North Carolina, there was one of the biggest rivers you've ever laid eyes on. It is called the Pamlico River. It led right out to the sound and eventually to the ocean. When I say big, it was probably more than a mile wide near my old, historic home. It was breathtaking and where I spent many hours of play and wonder. My cousins and I would pretend on its banks and swim on its shores most summer days. It was in these playful moments that I met my playful God. My love and connection to hearing God through creation is now an intricate part of my life. I don't know a single person who goes outside and spends more than five minutes out there without getting refreshed and feeling a sense of newness.

This year our world is walking out something we never have gone through before. COVID-19 hit hard. During quarantining and lots of days of isolation, being outdoors and enjoying God's voice in all He made was a lifeline. In chapters 1 and 2 of Genesis, we find the ultimate epic story of a creative God having the best time of His life, getting His hands dirty and messy, releasing the colors and passions and desires of His heart. He put His whole heart into the masterpiece of earth and space. Then He went on to create the most beautiful, good thing, man and woman. I don't know about you, but there are moments when I go out for a walk with my kids or my husband, Cory, that I can almost hear the footsteps of my Creator beside us. His presence is so close in the wind, in the sound of the buzzing bee flying from flower to flower, in the smell of the rain as it falls from heaven, in the delight of the first snowflake falling on my nose. Genesis 3:8 tells us that Adam and Eve heard God walking in the cool of the day. A friend of mine, Matt Gilman, wrote a song back in our IHOP–KC days, and the chorus goes like this, "To walk in the cool of the day with you, to gaze on the beauty of all you do, to meditate on your glorious splendor, I was made for you."

Creation is a glorious gift bestowed to us by our Maker, and just as He was there in the garden, waiting to walk and talk with Adam and Eve, He is still very alive and ready to walk, talk, and display His glory to us.

> *For since the creation of the world God's invisible qualities—his eternal power and divine nature—have been clearly seen, being understood from what has been made, so that they are without excuse. (Romans 1:20)*

Did you read that? Go back and read it again! It is saying that in the creation of the world, all the invisible parts of God can be seen; therefore, everyone has a chance to get to know the eternal power of the Godhead through creation. If the lost soul can see and hear Him through His creation, how much more can we as sons and daughters hear His voice and see His invisible attributes through all He has made?

Often when Cory is asked where He connects the most with the Father, he responds simply, "When I'm alone fishing." It isn't when he's leading worship, although he's had some incredible God moments there. It isn't while he's writing a song or even reading the Word. For Cory, the voice of God is strongest in the beautiful outdoors with his fishing pole and lure, hunting for the big one that got away last time, and enjoying the rest and presence of His father outside.

Your Father, the ultimate Craftsman, made a massive playground called creation for you. Whether it's taking a hike, skiing, snow tubing down a hill, climbing trees, going for a swim in the dead of summer, the fun is endless, the connection with Him limitless. You can hear Him speaking through it all! I encourage you even now to take a break and go explore the gift of creation. The Father is smiling, laughing, and anticipating your arrival.

Hearing through Community

Psalm 34:8 encourages us to *"taste and see that the Lord is good; blessed is the one who takes refuge in him."* I love that God created food. Food is one of the great delights of daily life. You may be thinking, *What does food have to do with friendship and hearing God?* Well, my dear friend, so much, so very much.

About ten years ago, Cory and I began to develop times of feasting together with our worship team, close friends, and family. These moments have become some of the dearest memories and times I can remember. Jesus chose to perform His first miracle at a wedding with dear friends. He broke bread with His disciples and taught them on a normal basis. Eating together and enjoying one another were activities Jesus and His disciples were doing on a normal basis.

Most of Jesus' life, however, was lived in secret. From twelve years of age into His thirties, the monologue of His life was silent. I love to daydream about what this time was like. Jesus was a real human. He did chores for his mother, played with his siblings, and probably learned his father Joseph's trade as a carpenter. He lived our life—the mundane, the joyful, the hard, and the normal. He walked through it all, and it was sacred. He had dinner at nights with His beloved family, and more than likely He helped His mother make the meals or at least set the table. It was in this beautiful in-between time that Jesus cultivated a life of intimacy and prayer with His Father. It was in these moments, the hidden and unseen, that Jesus prepared Himself for three short years of ministry. He didn't suddenly start learning how to communicate with the Father while He was doing miracles. No way! He had grown in relationship with His Father through all the moments of life that we find ourselves in as well.

Jesus submitted Himself to the process and community of family, and it was there that He *"grew in wisdom and stature, and in favor with God and man"* (Luke 2:52). At the culmination of this hidden time, He was baptized by John, His cousin, and the voice of the Father thundered from heaven, *"This is my Son; with him I am well pleased!"* (Matt. 3:17). The Father wasn't pleased with all the miracles and teachings Jesus had been doing, because He hadn't performed or spoken a single word yet. The Father was proud because of how Jesus had grown and chosen faithfulness in the middle of family and community.

When we look at the life of Jesus, we see the fruit and abundance of His hearing His Father in all circumstances. There is a reflection of this rhythm in His three years of ministry that we get a small glimpse of through the Gospels. Jesus spent many hours eating with friends and sinners: Mary and Martha, Lazarus, the disciples, the disciples' families, weddings, the Jewish feasts, Zacchaeus, and the list goes on and on. He was also found in the synagogue, teaching and asking questions. All places where people were gathered to worship. Yes, I am referring to feasting and dining together as worship. There are moments when we sing, shout, and pray together. There are also moments where we eat, laugh, and remember together. So, how can we hear God through community?

We can hear Him through community in many ways. You can hear Him through a vulnerable text to a friend who texts you back the verse you've been needing to hear. Through dinner with friends where you laugh harder than you have all week, and you remember that God is good. On a coffee date while you hear the stories of a friend's life and remember God's faithfulness and thank Him for friendship. Through a Sunday morning church service where you sing and shout until you again believe that what He said He would do, He will do. Connection to community is key in hearing the voice of God. We need each other, and we need to hear from one another the ways He is speaking to us individually.

Cory and I have a few good, deep friendships, and we are almost daily in a conversation through texting, calling, dinner, etc., cheering each other on, praying for one another, laughing about things, and reminding each other how far we've come. Without these friends, I'm sure we would have gone off course several times. Friendship is good for the soul, and without community it is going to be close to impossible to walk out this journey of life in the fullness of what it was meant to be.

Outro

I hope as you read this chapter from Anna you were inspired in your desire to hear God's voice in your life. I hope you received vision and encouragement to try some of these tools she gave you. Maybe new ideas came to you as you read, or maybe you were reminded of old tools you haven't used in a while. It's time to activate these ideas in your life and put into practice these disciplines. Our relational God desires fellowship and communion with you. He is waiting for you!

Closing Prayer

Pray this prayer with me over yourself. It may help to read it aloud.

Father,
Would you give me eyes to see and ears to hear what the Spirit is saying. Would you give me ears to hear Your voice like Samuel, that I would know Your voice louder and greater than all the other voices trying to get my attention. Let Your voice speak identity over me. Let hunger arise in my heart to know You more and to live by every word that comes from Your mouth.
    Speak, Lord, Your servant is listening.
    Amen.

Prompt

Take time to go on a walk. It can be alone or with friends, but make sure the purpose of your walk is to hear God speaking through His creation. You don't have to be super serious or even quiet. Don't overthink it. Go out ready to be surprised and encountered however God wants to show up. It could be through the breeze or in the sound of a bird chirping. Maybe, if it's the winter, it could be through the peacefulness of falling snow. Whatever the way, He's speaking, and He's waiting to speak to you through His creation.

After you walk, come back and write down in your journal what He spoke to you while you were on your walk. The moments He speaks you want to remember, and you want to be able to go back and read what He said again.

A Testimony

Our testimony with prophetic worship ministry goes back years as I have been blessed many times by this ministry. But recently my wife and I had undergone a really hard transition. We were thrust out of a church culture and community and employment really suddenly. We relocated and went through so much change in a short period of time. As we were trying to wrap our heads around the last difficult season, we came across a prophetic song from an online conference. Though it wasn't recorded for me, and I wasn't in the room for the recording, the Lord worked through it, and it ministered so deeply to us.

A myriad of the things sung in the song spoke to us. Phrase after phrase gave us the Lord's perspective on those hard years. We heard Him say through the singer, "You didn't waste your time when you wasted it on Me," "all those years were such a gift to Me," and "Let Me be enough.

I didn't even know I needed to hear these things, but the phrases were so specific to us and speaking to us in our current season.

—Carson

Developing Biblical Language

Your word is a lamp for my feet, a light on my path. (Psalm 119:105)

In the last chapter, Anna highlighted the idea of hearing God's voice through His Word as one of the ways we can hear Him speak. We will inevitably learn the language of His Word as we pursue His voice in our lives.

The language of prophetic songs is the language that God speaks. He has given us His Word in book form as a gift, and this gift is meant to be our meditation. We need to be reading the Bible for our own growth and development in our relationship with Jesus. What will be a byproduct of that is we will learn the Bible. We will learn more of who God is and what He sounds like, what His tone is; we will learn His emotions and His heart. We will be filled with His Word and then able to declare it in song because it has been written inside us.

> **He has given us His Word in book form as a gift, and this gift is meant to be our meditation.**

Imagine being sent by your king to a distant land to tell the people a message from him. You get up in the middle of the town square to share the message when, suddenly, you realize you don't know the message. And as you think about it, you barely know the king. How can you deliver a message from the king accurately when you don't know him, how he speaks, and what he wants to say?

Know the Man

Sometimes, God asks us to share what is on His heart with a person or a group of people. We must know Him personally and intimately before we can share His heart with others.

This next story might be even more scary than the first one about the king and his message. Imagine being sent by the king to a distant land to tell the people a message from the king. You get up in the middle of the town square to share his message, and instead, you share your own message. It doesn't seem to bother you that you don't know the king. Sure, you've met him once or twice, but you don't know what he sounds like or what he is passionate about. *It doesn't matter*, you begin to think, as you are a very gifted public speaker and have your own opinions and things to say.

> **We will learn more of who God is and what He sounds like, what His tone is; we will learn His emotions and His heart. We will be filled with His Word and then able to declare it in song because it has been written inside us.**

After every message you give, the people always surround you and praise you for the message and the way you strung phrases together and developed the ideas. You beam with delight and barely recognize the truth that the king didn't even give you a message. You are celebrated for your gifting. The townspeople have heard and seen your gift, but sadly they have not heard the message their king was longing to give them.

Our King, the King of kings, has messages, words, and songs to give to us. They were written into 66 canonized books of the Bible. We so easily ignore what God is longing to say. You might struggle with that sentence and say, "Rachel, that is so not true. I am desperate for God to speak to me and my situation. I am not ignoring His voice." But you have ignored the written Word of God at times, haven't you? Haven't we all? And that book is full of His voice and words that He wants to speak to us today.

Psalm 119:11 speaks to the idea of hiding God's Word in our hearts. He wants us to embark on the beautiful journey of allowing the Word to lodge deep in our hearts. We must believe that God wants to speak to us through the Bible. And we must believe that He will. If we read it to fulfill religious obligations or just because we think we should, we are only checking boxes and doing dead works.

> **Reading the Bible is not about religion or checking a box that you read your Bible. It is all unto relationship and encounter. The discipline of reading your Bible sets you up to fall more in love with Jesus and His ways.**

As Anna mentioned in the last chapter, Hebrews 4:12 tells us God's Word is alive. It is not stagnant, boring, or lifeless, but it is active!

The *Logos* Word of God is always speaking. And we have unlimited access to it. Oh, that His Word would be our delight and not our naptime reading material. We want to be people who delight in His Word, day and night:

> *Blessed is the man who walks not in the counsel of the ungodly, nor stands in the path of sinners, nor sits in the seat of the scornful;* ***but his delight is in the law of the Lord, and in His law he meditates day and night.*** *(Psalm 1:1–2 NKJV)*

Read the Bible

There are plenty of helpful tools out there to help you get started reading the Bible. Read the Bible in a year, read a chapter of Proverbs every day of the month, read slowly, read quickly, and meditate on one phrase. Read the same passage in multiple versions. Choose a modern translation like *The Message* or *The Passion Translation* to change it up.

Through my own walk with Jesus, I have done variations of all these ideas. I've seen different seasons of life promote different styles and paces of reading.

I remember at the start of 1999 I decided as a fifteen-year-old to endeavor to read through the Bible in a year. I found a chart that measured out suggested reading for every day, and I went for it. I think I saw reading the Bible in its entirety in a year as an opportunity to grow in my relationship with the Lord, but I couldn't have imagined the way it set me up for a lifetime of diving into the Truth and the heart of God. The Bible became alive. I couldn't wait to read it. I had a three-ring binder that I would pull out, and as I read, if any verses stuck out to me, I would write them down in the binder along with my prayer list. I wish I still had that binder. It contained my journey with Jesus that year. It held all the verses that spoke to me and all the things I was talking to Jesus about.

I also remember the seasons of life right after my children were born. I remember countless sleepless nights and days going by where I couldn't remember the last time I ate a meal or read a full chapter in my Bible. During these times, I would cling to a verse. Usually, those verses were something like David's cry for help in Psalm 86. Simple phrases of Scripture carried me during these times, phrases like, "Show me a sign of your goodness," "You help me and comfort me," "Teach me what you want me to do," "You are great and you do miracles," "You answer me," "Lord, you are kind and forgiving," "Answer me," and "Help me!" That last phrase isn't in Psalm 86, but it is one of my all-time favorites along with other simple phrases from Psalm 86.

Reading the Bible is not about religion or checking a box that you read your Bible. It is all unto relationship and encounter. The discipline of reading your Bible sets you up to fall more in love with Jesus and His ways.

Natasha, a dear friend of mine, is one of the most disciplined people I know personally in reading the Bible. Every day she reads ten chapters. If she had a late night last night, next morning—ten chapters. If she was up all night with her kids who were sick, next morning—ten chapters. When she's got it all together and her life is in order, she reads ten chapters. When she had cancer and was very sick, she read ten chapters.

This may sound like religion to you or rigid, but the other part about Natasha that I want to mention is her unwavering love and faith in Jesus. In her disciplined lifestyle to read the Bible, she has grown more in love with Jesus and with the Word. She reads the Word now because she recognizes that it is truly what sustains her and gives her life. She has been digesting the Word of God for years. It's inside her. When she sings and leads worship, Scripture just pours out of her mouth. Every prophetic song she has sung and declared has been dripping with fresh revelation straight from the Word of God.

This lifestyle of discipline in our relationship with Jesus should provoke us to step out and dive into routines, habits, and rhythms that encourage growth in our spiritual disciplines. I included lyrics from a worship set where Natasha sang a prophetic song. Notice the language. Do you recognize any scripture verses gracing this song? There are direct word-for-word verses as well as multiple inferences.

Prophetic Song True North 2020
Natasha Downs and Radiant City Music

The entirety of this prophetic song can be heard on the audiobook.

> *You've been working, fighting against my love*
> *You've been working, striving, fighting against my love*
> *You are growing weary, weary in the fight*
> *Today I am causing you to lie down in green pastures*
> *You don't have to fight anymore*
> *You don't have to strive anymore*
> *Lie down, lie down*
> *It's time to receive. It's time to receive maybe for the first time*
> *It's time to believe. It's time to believe maybe for the first time*
> *And I'm breaking those lies over you*
> *I am coming with truth today, right now.*
> *You are wanted*
> *You are chosen*
> *You are accepted.*

It's time to receive. It's time to believe in His love for you.
Look up, look up, it's a banner of love over you.
We receive His love

I don't have to fight for your attention, earn your affection
I already have it, I already have it.
I look up, look up, it's a banner of love over me.

Don't Just Read the Bible, Talk to Jesus

I want to challenge you as you read and study the Word of God to dialogue with Jesus as you read. Ask Him questions about His heart. Ask Him what passages mean. My favorite prayer from the apostolic prayers is from Ephesians 1:17–18: *"that the God of our Lord Jesus Christ, the Father of glory, may give to you the spirit of wisdom and revelation in the knowledge of Him, the eyes of your understanding being enlightened"* (NKJV).

When I read the Bible, I am also asking for revelation on what I am reading. I ask for words to jump off the page and for sections that were once confusing to me to suddenly be clear. The Bible can be a launching pad into new conversations with Jesus.

For example, while reading Psalm 23, I could ask the Lord how He wants to be my Shepherd and my Leader during this season of my life. I could thank Him for leading me so perfectly. I could tell Him that I feel like I am walking in the valley of the shadow of death and ask Him to show me again that He is with me. I could ask Him to reveal to my heart what the green pastures and still waters look like in my own life. The list goes on of the ways we could dive into conversation (prayer) around the passages of Scripture we are reading.

Write the Bible

Since you are reading this book, my guess is that you have done some reading of the Bible, and I probably don't need to convince you it's a good idea. So, what I want to share with you next is that there are more ways to get the Word of God inside you.

Back in school, particularly high school, I learned the value of writing notes when the teacher was lecturing. I would also take notes when I was reading my textbooks. Most of the time, I would write down word for word important parts of the textbook. This would help me remember the content and prepared me for tests.

Similarly, writing down the verse or verses you are meditating on can help you slow down and take in the content. You typically can't write as fast as you can read. The act of writing causes you to slow down. As you read through a familiar psalm, you may notice one verse in particular that stands out to you. Instead of moving on, write that verse down. Maybe as you write the verse down, more thoughts and ideas on the same subject come to mind. Begin to write those down as well. Write down your meditative thoughts on the verse. Pray Ephesians 1:17, asking for the spirit of revelation as you read through a passage. As God begins to speak and highlight an idea or a word, write it down.

Memorize the Bible

Psalm 119:11 tells us, *"Your word I have hidden in my heart, that I might not sin against You"* (NKJV). What does it mean to hide the Word in your heart? What does it mean to truly know the Scriptures?

My daughter Aaliyah is eight years old, and we have her in a classical learning environment where she is learning foundational history, English, and science facts through memorization. I have been blown away during this process by her ability to memorize and store data in long-term memory storage. She is rattling off state capitals, times tables, history facts, and Bible verses. And it hasn't been burdensome for her. She is enjoying it!

When I was young, my parents had me memorize 2 Timothy 3:15.

> *And that from childhood you have known the Holy Scriptures, which are able to make you wise for salvation through faith which is in Christ Jesus. (NKJV)*

They truly believed this verse and desired for me to know the Scriptures. So, I spent my early years memorizing verses and then full chapters of the Bible. I am now in my thirties, and I can say I still have those verses and chapters mostly memorized. I didn't realize then as a kid with all these verses stored in my head the way they would slowly implant into my heart throughout the years. I had truth inside me. These verses and passages shaped my worldview. They grounded me in truth. These verses would resurface years after not thinking about a particular passage, but the Holy Spirit would bring it to remembrance from the deep recesses of my long-term memory (see John 14:26). The truth that was hidden away would move me again and bring peace.

This discipline is not so we can say we have the Bible memorized. The Word of God is our food. It sustains us and brings life to our souls.

Sing the Bible

Read the Bible out loud, and go a step further—sing it! When I was about fourteen, I used to sit at my piano, open up to a passage of Scripture, and begin to sing the Scripture to a chord progression I would play on the piano. These times with the Word of God were very precious to me. I wrote many mini songs to some of my favorite Scripture verses. The melodies were simple, and the lyrics were typically word-for-word Scripture. What felt so significant about these times was the way my emotions would come alive and be engaged with the Word.

Singing and music unlock our emotions. They help us feel, and they can set the tone or atmosphere of a room or a heart. I would feel and be emotionally present during those times of singing Scripture unlike some of the times when I would read the Word without singing and making melody. When you spontaneously sing Scripture, you have the opportunity to elaborate, not only on the words or "lyrics," but on the feel and tone.

Take a moment and try this on your own. Write a mini song set to the lyrics of your favorite verse or the verse God has been speaking to you. Sing it to the Lord.

Pray the Bible

Prayer, put simply, is a conversation with God. God wants to have a dialogue with you. He wants to communicate with you, and He also wants you to talk with Him.

First Thessalonians 5:16–19 says, *"Rejoice always,* ***pray continually****, give thanks in all circumstances; for this is God's will for you in Christ Jesus."*

As we read the Word, we can also pray the Word. We can agree with His Word and tell Him our agreement in our own words. We can ask questions about the content, or we can use His Word as a launching pad into conversation.

We can also pray prayers that are in the Bible. The Bible is filled with prayers prayed by the saints. It is filled with desperate prayers, prophetic prayers, prayers for favor, prayers for safety and rescue, prayers for self, prayers for others, and so on.

Here is a short list of some of my favorite prayers from the Bible. This list is by no means exhaustive. Go ahead and right now, pray one of these prayers. Pray it over yourself, your family, your church or your city.

> *"Our Father in heaven, Hallowed be Your name. Your kingdom come. Your will be done on earth as it is in heaven. Give us this day our daily bread. And forgive us our debts, as we forgive our debtors. And do not lead us into temptation, but deliver us from the evil one. For Yours is the kingdom and the power and the glory forever. Amen." (Matthew 6:9b–13 NKJV)*

> *Lord . . . grant to Your servants that with all boldness they may speak Your word, by stretching out Your hand to heal, and that signs and wonders may be done through the name of Your holy Servant Jesus. And when they had prayed, the place where they were assembled together was shaken; and they were all filled with the Holy Spirit, and they spoke the word of God with boldness. (Acts 4:29–31)*

In the last days, says God, that I will pour out of My Spirit on all flesh; your sons and your daughters shall prophesy, Your young men shall see visions, your old men shall dream dreams. On My menservants and on My maidservants I will pour out My Spirit in those days; and they shall prophesy. I will show wonders in heaven above and signs in the earth beneath: blood, fire and vapor of smoke. The sun shall be turned into darkness, and the moon into blood, **before** *the coming of the great and awesome day of the Lord. Whoever calls on the name of the* Lord *shall be saved. (Acts 2:17–21)*

May the God of patience and comfort grant you to be like-minded toward one another... that you may with one mind and one mouth glorify the . . . Father. . . . May the God of hope fill you with all joy and peace in believing, that you may abound in hope by the power of the Holy Spirit. (Romans 15:5–6, 13)

"That the Father of glory, may give to you the spirit of wisdom and revelation in the knowledge of Him, the eyes of your understanding being enlightened; that you may know what is the hope of His calling, what are the riches of the glory of His inheritance in the saints, and what is the exceeding greatness of His power toward us who believe, according to the working of His mighty power." (Ephesians 1:17–19 NKJV)

"That He would grant you, according to the riches of His glory, to be strengthened with might through His Spirit in the inner man, that Christ may dwell in your hearts through faith; that you, being rooted and grounded in love, may be able to comprehend with all the saints what is the width and length and depth and height—to know the love of Christ which passes knowledge; that you may be filled with all the fullness of God." (Ephesians 3:16–19 NKJV)

"That your love may abound still more and more in knowledge and all discernment, that you may approve the things that are excellent, that you may be sincere and without

offense till the day of Christ, being filled with the fruits of righteousness."(Philippians 1:9–11 NKJV)

"That you may be filled with the knowledge of His will in all wisdom and spiritual understanding; that you may have a walk worthy of the Lord, fully pleasing Him, being fruitful in every good work and increasing in the knowledge of God; strengthened with all might, according to His glorious power, for all patience and longsuffering with joy." (Colossians 1:9–11 NKJV)

"Pray for us, that the word of the Lord may run swiftly and be glorified, just as it is with you and that we may be delivered... But the Lord is faithful, who will establish you and guard you from the evil one... Now may the Lord direct your hearts into the love of God and into the patience of Christ." (2 Thessalonians 3:1–5 NKJV)

Other Practical Ways to Develop Biblical Language

Throughout this chapter, we have identified ways in which we grow in our knowledge of God through His Word and through praying, singing, and writing His Word. All these things help us develop biblical language for prophetic speaking, praying, and singing. But there are some other practical ways you can develop biblical language as a prophetic singer.

Repeat the Word

There is power in the Word of God. The simplest and maybe the most powerful way to develop in prophetic singing is to repeat or sing what the Scripture says. As we become more and more accustomed to singing the Word, this part tends to be the most neglected. Sometimes, the simple things are the hardest to do. In our search for biblical language, or our own heart language, we can forget the power of simply repeating back the Bible. So, here's what I recommend you do.

Repeat the phrases of the Word that you're reading slowly. Let the truth of the words wash over you. Then repeat them again. Don't move on quickly from these moments of simplicity. There is power in the washing of the water of the Word. Feel the words touch your soul. Allow the truth to hit your heart. There is opportunity here for the Scriptures to come alive in your heart. It is in these moments that truth sinks in. We are changed and transformed by this slow process of allowing the Word to wash over us as Ephesians 5:25–27 says,

> *Just as Christ loved the church and gave himself up for her to make her holy,* **cleansing her by the washing with water through the word,** *and to present her to himself as a radiant church, without stain or wrinkle or any other blemish, but holy and blameless.*

The plan of God is to have His Bride be presented in the end as holy and blameless. This process of sanctification is closely knit to the reality of the Word of God being what cleanses and washes us. The result of us giving into the process of letting the Word of God hit our hearts is our personal sanctification. In the end, we are made holy just as He is holy.

Put It in Your Own Words

Another way to say this is to rephrase the original text using your own language. Can you put it in your own words? Your understanding of the passage will increase if you can rephrase it. This will help expand your heart language. You can ask yourself what today's passage, for example, may be speaking to you.

Tie It into Another Passage!

The fancy word for this is *cross-referencing*. Use other passages of Scripture to bring in more biblical content and support the ideas of the original passage. This tool grows as we become more familiar with the

Word. Passages we have read in the past or heard our pastor preach will suddenly connect with what we are reading today.

Journal through a Passage

I am going to give you an example of one of my journal entries where I dove into Psalm 23. For months the Lord was highlighting this chapter to me and speaking to me from the phrases in this chapter. So, I took some time and asked the Lord for revelation on His Word and what He wanted to speak to me through His Word.

There are moments of vulnerability in this journal entry that I am honored to share with you. So, welcome to my heart and welcome to a window into one of my conversations with God. I hope that it encourages you to dive into the world of journaling, but I also hope you see the way the Bible can be used to have conversation and intimacy with the Father. The language in the Bible is beautiful, poetic, raw, and true. It is the Holy Spirit-inspired Word of God given to us as a gift, and this gift is for our sustenance, refreshment, and restoration.

Psalm 23

You are my Shepherd

You are the one who really sees me and takes care of me. You know my needs and anticipate my struggles and weaknesses. You are not shocked by them or disappointed. You are right with me every step of the way, gently leading and guiding my steps. I am so moved by Your tenderness toward me today. Your unconditional love for me and desire to see me whole is incomprehensible. I can be so flippant and distracted, dishonoring Your presence and focused on my own selfish desires, yet still You are gently and tenderly leading me.

I shall not want

Everything I need is found in You. Help me believe that. You are my Source. Jesus, be my everything, like the old Vineyard song that we sang at True North a couple days ago, "Jesus be the center, be my source, be my guide, Jesus." There are some deep longings and wants of my heart, Father. I want so deeply to have my son develop into the fullest and healthiest expression of himself possible on this side of eternity. I feel so needy. I am standing today on Your Word that says, "My God shall supply all your needs according to His riches in glory by Christ Jesus" (Phil. 4:19 NKJV). Would You give my family everything we need to walk in righteousness and love? Would You give me peace today?

You make me lie down in green pastures and lead me beside still waters

Father, would You do that today? This doesn't look like a green pasture, and it doesn't feel like still water. It feels more like a storm and my tiny little boat has holes. It feels like I'm sinking. Would You lead me to a place of rest? Help me find my rest in You. Help me let go of my worry.

At the end of this chapter, I have left a few prompts for you. Take some time this week to dive into these prompts. Take the opportunity to speak to God about His Word. Ask Him what He wants to share with you through the passage. Most importantly, listen for His voice and write down what He speaks to you.

Closing Prayer

Pray this prayer with me. It may help to read it aloud.

Father,

I ask that our delight would be to meditate on Your Word. Like Psalm 1 says, we want to meditate on it day and night. Oh, that we would recognize the Word of God is what sustains us. Just one word from You shatters every lie. One word from You gives hope to a hopeless situation. One word from You brings life to the dead places in our hearts. We need Your Word written inside us.

As we come to grips with our need for Your Word and for Your voice in our lives, would You give us the grace to dive into Scripture? We want to want to read the Word. Help us and teach us how to eat and consume Your Word. Give us the tools we need. Would You cause words to jump off the page? Would You highlight and illuminate Your Word to us? Give us a spirit of wisdom and revelation as we read. Open our eyes and our hearts to Your truth.

I ask for the very busy soul who is reading this book—the one who just can't seem to find the time, would You strengthen them inside to slow down and meditate? The Mom with babies strapped to her while homeschooling slews of children, the businessman or businesswoman who greatly desires to dive into the Scriptures but can't seem to find a rhythm of study, the singer or musician who hasn't yet discovered the life-giving power of the written Word of God—would You encounter my friend as he or she sits down to do the following prompts? Would he or she not find a desert, but a spring of life?

Father, we thank You for Your written Word. We believe it is living and active. We believe that You still speak through Your Word and are longing to encounter our souls through the reading of that Word. Meet us today in Your Word.

Amen.

Prompt 1

Choose one verse or a small passage that you feel the Holy Spirit has been bringing to your remembrance lately. If you are having trouble choosing, one of my favorites right now is Psalm 27:4. Remember, this prompt is meant only as a launching pad for you into studying the Word of God and letting it transform you.

Read the Passage

First, read the passage. Take your time, and maybe read it a few times.

Write the Passage

Secondly, write the passage down on paper. I write mine right in my journal when I do this exercise.

Say the Passage

Next, say the passage out loud.

Memorize the Passage

For this step, I urge you not to cram it into your short-term memory and memorize it for ten minutes and forget it entirely tomorrow. Quiz yourself in a few hours, tomorrow, and at the end of the week.

Sing the Passage

Have some fun with this one. Find a melody you enjoy singing. If you play an instrument, try playing a chord progression, and sing your melody to it. Try to match the feel of the passage with the feel of the music in your mini song. If there is strong emotion in the words, sing with strong emotion.

Pray the Passage

Pray the passage. Ask questions, wait for answers.

Journal the Passage

Lastly, write out what you learned from the passage and what God spoke to you through His Word.

Prompt 2

In this prompt, you are going to engage with lines from Psalm 23:1–3.

> *The Lord is my Shepherd, I shall not want. He makes me lie down in green pastures; He leads me beside still waters. He restores my soul. (NKJV)*

"The Lord Is My Shepherd"

Repeat this phrase and remember not to rush this step. Slow down and think about what this phrase means.

> *The Lord is my Shepherd*

Use your own words. What does this mean to you today? (Examples: "God, You are my tender Leader; You are the Keeper of my soul; You know me better than I know myself; You are my Provider, my Source of strength.")

What are some specific cross-references for the phrase that speak the same message to your heart?

"I Shall Not Want"

Repeat this phrase and remember not to rush this step. Slow down and think about what this phrase means.

> *I shall not want*

Use your own words. What does this mean to you today?
(Examples: "I will not lack; You are the giver of life; You will provide for me; I can trust You; You love to give.")

What are some specific cross-references for the phrase that speak the same message to your heart?

"He Makes Me Lie Down in Green Pastures"

Repeat this phrase and remember not to rush this step. Slow down and think about what this phrase means.

> *He makes me lie down in green pastures*

Use your own words. What does this mean to you today?
What are some specific cross-references for the phrase that speak the same message to your heart?

"He Leads Me beside Still Waters"

Repeat this phrase and remember not to rush this step. Slow down and think about what this phrase means.

> *He leads me beside still waters*

Use your own words. What does this mean to you today?

What are some specific cross-references for the phrase that speak the same message to your heart?

"He Restores My Soul"

Repeat this phrase and remember not to rush this step. Slow down and think about what this phrase means.

He restores my soul

Use your own words. What does this mean to you today?

What are some specific cross-references for the phrase that speak the same message to your heart?

Write out a sincere prayer to the Lord, using the themes, ideas, and references that were highlighted to you during these meditations, whether it be thankfulness, questions, requests, etc. Take your time with this. Leave space in the middle or at the end for the Lord to speak back to you. Write His voice back to you! He wants to speak, so remember to give Him space. Don't second guess what He says; just write it down!

Prompt 3

In this prompt, you are going to engage with Psalm 27:1—*"The Lord is my light and my salvation—whom shall I fear? The Lord is the stronghold of my life—of whom shall I be afraid?"*

"The Lord Is My Light"

Repeat this phrase and remember not to rush this step. Slow down and think about what this phrase means.

> *The Lord is my light*

Use your own words. What does this mean to you today?

What are some specific cross-references for the phrase that speak the same message to your heart?

"And My Salvation"

Repeat this phrase and remember not to rush this step. Slow down and think about what this phrase means.

> *And my salvation*

Use your own words. What does this mean to you today?

What are some specific cross-references for the phrase that speak the same message to your heart?

"Whom Shall I Fear?"

Repeat this phrase and remember not to rush this step. Slow down and think about what this phrase means.

Whom shall I fear?

Use your own words. What does this mean to you today?

What are some specific cross-references for the phrase that speak the same message to your heart?

"The Lord Is the Stronghold of My Life"

Repeat this phrase and remember not to rush this step. Slow down and think about what this phrase means.

The Lord is the stronghold of my life

Use your own words. What does this mean to you today?

What are some specific cross-references for the phrase that speak the same message to your heart?

"Of Whom Shall I Be Afraid?"

Repeat this phrase and remember not to rush this step. Slow down and think about what this phrase means.

Of whom shall I be afraid?

Use your own words. What does this mean to you today?

What are some specific cross-references for the phrase that speak the same message to your heart?

Write out a sincere prayer to the Lord, using the themes, ideas, and references that were highlighted to you during these meditations, whether it be thankfulness, questions, requests, etc. Take your time with this. Leave space in the middle or at the end for the Lord to speak back to you. Write His voice back to you! He wants to speak so remember to give Him space. Don't second guess what He says; just write it down!

A Testimony

I was in one of my church's prayer meetings during our 21 days of prayer and fasting. During the meeting, the Lord was working on my heart in the area of deeply rooted insecurity as I questioned my season of life (e.g., job, living situation, relationships). During a moment of hearing the Lord personally, one of the singers began to sing out these words: "These past two years were not a mistake. You heard the Lord speak, and you followed Him and obeyed. It didn't look like you thought it would, and at times you felt abandoned, but He was right there in it the whole time!"

I felt like she must have been hearing the conversation I was having with the Lord; I knew that this song was for me. The beautiful thing about prophetic songs is that they may have been for other people in the room, too!

Something massively shifted in my life that night. My heart was broken open to the love and care of my Heavenly Father who had been in it with me for two years of life changes and beyond!

I came home and wrote it all down, and I love to go back now and read the words of that prophetic song that was sung from the Father to me.

—Haley

Prophetic Song

Ephesians 5:19 says we are to speak *"to **one another** in psalms and hymns and spiritual songs, singing and making melody in [our hearts] to the Lord."* This command Paul gave us is for everyone in the Church! He didn't say that leaders are to be the only ones singing the songs. He didn't say, "Worship leaders, sing something spiritual while everyone else takes a coffee break." We are *all* called to be filled with the Holy Spirit and engage in singing psalms, hymns, and spiritual songs. Engaging in prophetic singing is for everybody!

Psalms

When Paul mentioned psalms in Ephesians 5:19, he was simply referring to the Bible. I talked a lot about that in the chapter on developing biblical language and hearing God's voice through Scripture. Paul was talking about the books of the Bible that they had at that time: the books of the law, also called the Pentateuch, and the prophets and the literal Psalms. Paul was basically saying, *"Sing the Bible!"* He was telling us to use the language that is in the inspired Word of God and declare it.

Hymns

The hymns Paul mentioned are songs crafted by man. Hymns in this verse are not referring to the songs in our modern-day hymnals. Hymns refers to *all* the songs that man writes. What a gift these songs are to the Body of Christ. Every week, churches across America and the world are choosing songs for their setlist to lead congregations into worship. We have songs for so many themes, songs that speak of the cross, songs about the resurrection, songs that stir faith. We have songs that tell Jesus we love Him and so on. Our songwriters are writing incredible worship songs, and we all get to sing them!

There is one thing these professional songwriters can't write for us, and that is the expression of our hearts to the Lord in every moment with our own words and with our own voices. God loves our worship. He is glorified in these man-made songs, but He wants something more. He wants our words of worship.

Spiritual Songs

Let's say Valentine's Day is approaching, like it does every February 14th. I am scrambling yet again to find the perfect card to express my love and affection for my spouse. I find a great card (which never happens, by the way, but let's just say I find *the* perfect one). I give it to my husband, Caleb. He opens it, and just to heap on the romance, I read it aloud to him. It's poetic, it's articulate, and it says what's in my heart better than I could say it myself—I mean, every word of it. He receives these words off the card, smiles, and feels my love and affection.

A few weeks pass, my husband asks me, "How do you feel about me today?" I tell him to wait a second, and I run to find the Valentine's Day card I gave him last month. I begin to read the words to him. He stops me mid-sentence and says, "I want to hear from you how you feel about me, with your own words." He is not negating the power of the words written for me to express my love, but he also wants to hear it from my own heart and my own articulation. He doesn't care that it won't rhyme. He doesn't care that it won't start with, "Roses are red, violets are blue." He is longing for the honest expression of my own heart with my own words.

God is longing for these words and songs from our own hearts, not just the Hallmark card songs someone wrote for us. Paul calls such songs *spiritual songs* in Ephesians 5:19. These songs are the spontaneous "I love You, Jesus," or the "Thank You, Jesus," that we sing in worship because we are overwhelmed by His kindness. These are the songs that are stirred up inside us in the moment. These are the songs that move into that idea of a prophetic song. At the end of this chapter, you will practice this idea of singing your own song to the Lord.

> **There is one thing these professional songwriters can't write for us, and that is the expression of our hearts to the Lord in every moment with our own words and with our own voices.**

Have you been in a worship service and your worship leader or pastor says something like, "Let's all sing our own song to the Lord"? Or maybe they say, "Lift up your voice!" These are moments, right in the middle of corporate worship, where our leaders and pastors are inviting us to participate in articulating our hearts to God. Some of us jump at the chance to make up melodies and sing our little hearts out to God. Others of us go into panic mode because no one is singing for us or telling us what to sing.

Going Off Script

What if we thought of our Sunday morning church expression of worship and our song setlists as a script, pre-written lines of what to say and when to say it. We are fed our lines, and we can enter into corporate expressions of worship because we all have the same script.

We read the words off the script. Some of us even have different scripts memorized. We love our scripts. And our scripts are tools. Sometimes, a writer writes a new script, and as a church body, we all begin to learn the new script together. The scripts are for our benefit. They help us articulate feeling. They help us by giving us descriptors and analogies to extol God and tell Him how we feel about Him. Scripts or songs help us praise the Lord by feeding us our lines.

But sometimes actors, as you know, "go off script." They improvise. It is so important that we deviate from the script sometimes, too! I want to share with you my first experience with prophetic singing. It was truly the first time I heard other singers on the stage with me sing off script.

Back in 2003, I visited IHOP–KC. At the time, they were leading 24 hours a day, 7 days a week worship and prayer. Worship and prayer teams were taking turns leading two-hour sets in which they would alternate worshipping and praying during the course of that time. I walked into the prayer room and listened to the worship teams lead worship and sing straight to Jesus. I was amazed as the

> **God is longing for these words and songs from our own hearts, not just the Hallmark card songs someone wrote for us.**

prophetic singers sang the Word of God, and it seemed as if they weren't even reading the verses as they sang them. I had a few friends who were on staff at the time who knew I had spent years leading worship back in my hometown of Lima, New York. I was approached by one of them who explained that the next worship team was short a singer and asked if I would join them for their worship set. Looking back, hindsight is 20/20, and I should have said *no*. But I figured why not? I thought it would be fun. I led worship all the time back home and thought it could be good to jump in as a backup singer.

As the set began, we spent some time singing known worship songs that I was familiar with, and I sang my little heart out. But then something different happened. We were no longer singing known worship songs. We were singing something else. And we were no longer singing in unison. Singers were taking turns singing, and I could tell they were referencing a psalm in the Bible. They were singing phrases and ideas that went along with the verse. It was remarkable. I panicked, closed my eyes, and tried to think of what I could sing. In those moments that followed, I came to grips with the hard reality that I didn't really know the Word of God like I thought I did. I came face to face with my own barrenness of personal language. I realized that without the pre-written words of a song, I didn't know what to say or sing to the Lord in worship. I also realized that I wanted to have the language that these other singers had. I wanted to be able to sing my own words, emotions, and affections.

We are all going to fall somewhere on this spectrum of comfortability in singing off script to the Lord. I had been a worship leader for years without participating in these moments. So, wherever you find yourself, it's okay! Start there!

Closing Prayer

Pray this with me. It may help to read it aloud.

Father,
Here I am. I want to sing prophetically. I want to sing the song of the Lord and unlock the prophetic gifting in me. I choose to step out in faith and sing. I won't withhold my heart language from You. I will sing my love and affection for You. I will use my own words. I will use the Scripture. I want to be a fountain overflowing with spontaneous melodies, phrases, and songs. Would You unlock the flow of language? Would You open my ears to hear new melodies and phrases? I want to sing the songs heaven is singing. Fill me with courage!
    Amen.

Prompt 1

Let's take some steps together to begin practicing singing prophetic songs. And yes, it's okay to practice the prophetic.

If you have the audiobook, directly following this chapter I have included three live band chord progressions. You can use them to practice this prompt. You could also use an instrument, play a simple chord progression yourself, and begin singing to the Lord using phrases from your chosen psalm. Singing acapella is always an option as well.

You could also attend a worship service that leaves space and room during worship for the congregation to lift up their own songs and melodies to the Lord.

Sing out a simple phrase to the Lord. Don't just think the phrase. Actually, use your vocal chords and sing the phrase to Him. It could be a simple *I love you*. Or maybe you are connected to your heart language, and you have multiple phrases to sing.

What I want you to experience is stepping out of the box. I want you to move away from your prewritten script and sing something to the Lord that comes straight from your heart. Then let it flow. More phrases will come as you continue to practice singing from your heart.

Prompt 2

Use Scripture to jumpstart singing a new song to the Lord. Take your prompt from chapter 4 on developing biblical language and choose either Psalm 23 or 27. If you have the audiobook, directly following this chapter I have included three live band chord progressions. You can use them to practice this prompt. You could also use an instrument, play a simple chord progression yourself, and begin singing to the Lord, using phrases from your chosen psalm. Singing acapella is always an option as well.

Sing the verse.

Then sing some of the phrases you wrote down.

Maybe new phrases or ideas will come to you. Sing those out as well.

Is there one phrase that encompasses the main idea? Or one melody hook that you keep coming back to? Use those to create a chorus and repeat your chorus over and over again!

A Testimony

It was the beginning of my first year at a worship internship in Colorado. Early one Monday morning, I attended a worship and prayer set. The entire set seemed to have a theme of belonging to the Lord. In one moment, the singer began to sing and declare that the Lord was attentive to our prayers and longings. It was at that moment that I felt my heart want to break free of my chest. Then all the singers began singing "ohs." No words, just "ohs." I felt the presence of the Lord in that moment as they sang and the closeness of Jesus like I never had experienced before. I felt God singing over me my own belonging—that I belonged to Him.

That same year in my worship internship, I experienced the joy of the Lord in worship. I remember the musicians playing a chord progression and one of the singers matching the melody with a prophetic chorus that broke through my own pride and ego and released freedom and grace to dance around like a fool in the presence of the Lord.

—Autumn

Prophetic Songs in a Corporate Context

This chapter just might be my favorite chapter in the book. But for some reason it has been the hardest one to write and the hardest one to introduce. Singing prophetic songs in a corporate context is something that I started doing about fifteen years ago. I have grown in this gifting and skill from that time forward. I feel excited yet sober to share insight and wisdom on this subject that has become such a huge part of my life. There isn't one correct way to do this. It's not a formula that can be taught. But there are principles and wisdom you can learn to apply to prophetic singing.

> I believe with all my heart that the Lord is calling prophetic singers and musicians to arise in this specific time period in history. I know this calling isn't just for me and an elite few. This is a calling for many.

I believe with all my heart that the Lord is calling prophetic singers and musicians to arise in this specific time period in history. I know this calling isn't just for me and an elite few. This is a calling for many. I believe the Lord wants to give our worship leaders and singers songs from heaven. I believe He is inviting many to activate their prophetic gifting and join it with their singing anointing.

This chapter is filled with numerous examples of prophetic songs that have been released corporately. Lyrics have been put into the book, but to experience the songs in their fullness, you can hear them on the audiobook.

Three Perspectives

There are typically three perspectives used in our prophetic songs. Our words to Jesus, God's words to us as His Church or to us individually, and lastly, declarations of truth.

Our Words to Jesus

These are songs where we are singing straight to God. They use "I" or "We." They are prayers to the Lord, responses to Him, songs of worship and praise, as well as songs of remembrance and thankfulness.

Example Song

Monday Morning Prayer Meeting (03.29.21)

> *I open up my heart*
> *I open up my heart*
> *To You again, to You again, for You again*
> *I look to You. I won't look to the left. I won't look to the right.*
> *Oh, my eyes are on You, Jesus*
> *So just open up my heart to wonder. Open up my heart to Your majesty.*
> *Open it up again*
> *Show me Your glory*

God's Words to Us

These are songs where the song is delivered from the perspective of the Lord. His words are sung to us, the Church.

Example Song

This prophetic song can be heard on the audiobook.
Seek Service at Radiant Church (01.29.20)

> *Kalamazoo, I spoke over you before even time began*
> *Kalamazoo, I spoke over you before even time began*
> *Kalamazoo, I spoke over you before time you are Mine*
> *It's time to take your place. It's time to wake up from sleep*
> *It's time to take your place. Wake up*
> *From the North to the South to the East to the West*
> *WAKE UP*

Declarations of Truth

It is not the room singing to God or God singing to us. This singing is a declaration of truth. This prophetic song can be heard in its entirety on the audiobook.

Example Song

9 a.m. Weekend Service at Radiant Church (08.23.20)

> *Peace settling in now*
> *Peace is settling in now*
> *Can you feel peace settling in now?*
> *Peace is settling in now*
> *Perfect peace is settling in now*
> *Peace is settling in now*
> *Peace settling in now*
> *Perfect peace*
> *'Cause your mind's been so busy*
> *Your heart's been so downcast*
> *Your mind's been so busy, busy, busy, busy*
> *Your heart's been so downcast*

That's where your vision's been
It's been down
That's where your eyes have been
They've been down
But right now,
Peace is settling in now
Peace is settling in now
Perfect peace
Perfect peace
And it is washing away, away
All anxiety you face
It's washing away, away, away
All the fears you face
Oh, the perfect peace
It's settling in now
And finally you can see His face
Peace is settling in now
Peace is settling in now
Perfect peace is settling in now
So, we settle into it
Perfect peace
Peace is settling in now

The 4 Rs

I want to share with you four practical steps as we take the deep dive into how to sing prophetically: request, receive, release and rest. I have broken down each R so we can take a closer look. All four steps are an important part of the process. It doesn't work to skip a step or to try and do them out of order. Remember each step is important. Let's look at request first.

Request

James 4:2 says, *"You do not have because you do not ask God."* Every once in a while, I get a prophetic song from the Lord out of the blue. This is rare for me. *When we slow down enough to ask, this is when we are slowed down enough to listen!*

Jesus told us, *"Ask and it will be given to you; seek and you will find; knock and the door will be opened to you"* (Matt. 7:7). One thing I have noticed throughout the decades of practicing this is, when I ask, He gives. I ask the Holy Spirit what He is wanting to say or do in a worship set, and I get a response. I will feel something or get a picture, sense, or phrase. Now, just because He shared doesn't necessarily mean I need to take the set into a ten-minute prophetic song, but it does mean as a leader that I watch and lead the people into what the Holy Spirit wants to do. If the Lord is saying He wants to release peace into His people, sometimes that might mean praying in the mic for the peace of God to come. Other times, I could just observe as the Lord shows up with peace without me doing anything! I could sing a phrase or two about His peace. And sometimes, I could sing a new chorus about the peace of God and help the room participate with where God is leading us. All we really need to learn to do is ask God some simple questions like:

- What do You want to say to Your people today?
- What truth do we need to be reminded of?
- What are You already saying that I can highlight?
- What are You saying?
- What are You doing in the hearts of Your people?

Ask Often

Ask God questions and then wait and listen. This is a discipline we should be practicing often with the Lord personally, not just when we are asking specifically for a worship set. Holy Spirit, what are You doing in my life? What are You speaking to me? What is it that You want me to focus on today? What are the areas in my life that You want to highlight? What is the scripture that You want to encourage me with today? This is how we grow in relationship with God. Moses was a friend of God. God spoke to Moses face to face as a man speaks to his friend (see Exod. 33:11). Imagine having that kind of relationship with God. I want to be a friend of God like Moses. God loves to speak to us. Do we love to listen?

Ask Before

Ask before the set, the week of, during prep, during rehearsal. It is important for us to have our spiritual antennae up. I prefer the analogy of our sailboat having the sail up. I have a painting up in my home I received a few years back as a gift. It is a painting of a sailboat on the waters with its sail high in the air. Every time I look at that painting, I am reminded to put up my spiritual sail and let the Holy Spirit lead. We want to catch the wind of the Spirit on our sails so we can follow His lead. We don't need to go against the wind and forge our own path when He is leading somewhere else.

So, during the week, this is what putting up our sail looks like:

- It looks like asking.
- It looks like listening.
- It looks like expecting to hear, see, or feel something from the Father's heart.

When a sail catches the wind, it is effortless. In our asking and in our listening, we do not need to strive. Let each of these be effortless. Let listening and asking be second nature so you can feel the wind blowing and connecting your sail to the movement of the Holy Spirit.

Ask During

There is a lot to think about and much to remember and do during our times of leading worship. As singers, musicians, and worship leaders, we are thinking about chord progressions, lyrics, and melodies; we are watching for cues, listening for cues, remembering the road map of the song. Thoughts rush through our heads. *Is this a double chorus, or are we heading into the bridge? The click, that horrible click! Why is that singer doubling my harmony? Don't forget to engage in worship yourself!* The list goes on and on of what can be holding our attention during these times. It's important to work on musicality and skill off the stage so, when we are on the stage, we can worship. As we grow in our skill, we can also ask during these times of worship where the Holy Spirit wants to lead us. This may be my favorite time to ask.

The Game Slowed Down

I went to a small, private, Christian school growing up. I loved to play sports, and at my school basketball was king. When I was in ninth grade, I got called up to play varsity. Before you become too impressed, let me share with you how small my school was. My graduating class was 32! I remember my first varsity basketball game in horrible flashbacks. The game was so fast. I remember one second getting passed the ball and just freezing. Our best player was wide open and asking for the ball. I can still see her eyes pleading with me to just pass the ball! As I began to slowly process my options, the defender stole the ball right out of my hands and ran down the court for an easy layup.

> God loves to speak to us. Do we love to listen?

I played junior high basketball in seventh and eighth grade and then jumped straight to varsity games. It felt like I didn't have time to make decisions or think through anything. I felt like I was a step behind during the entire game. I never knew how much time was on the shot clock or if I had been in the paint too long. There was so much to think about and remember. We had a zillion plays to remember; *Are we pressing right now? Where is the girl I'm supposed to be guarding?* If you have played sports before, I'm sure you can relate to this feeling.

Throughout my school years, I continued to play basketball on the same team. By the time I was a senior in high school, something happened. The game slowed down for me. I was aware of my team and the plays we were running. I could see the other team and could recognize which plays they were trying to run. The shot clock was running in my head, and I felt confident and aware of the game.

When it comes to being a singer, musician, or leader, you may feel like a freshman playing varsity ball with so much to think about, and you may feel like you don't have the bandwidth to ask and listen in a worship set. But let me encourage you. You will grow in skill and confidence, and the entire worship set will seem to slow down for you.

Here is another fun, true story from my life I don't get to share too often. Maybe it's because it is slightly embarrassing!

Bass on a Keyboard

I was twelve years old and was finally old enough to join the youth group at my church. I attended Sunday morning youth group, and these twelfth graders on the worship team were rockin' the corporate worship times with a full band, multiple singers, worship leaders, and even a saxophone player. And let me tell you something, they sounded GOOD! One Sunday after church, I got pulled aside by my youth pastor, and he said to me, "So, Rachel, the youth group lost its bass player, and we were thinking; you know how you have been taking piano lessons with my wife? Well, what if you played bass on the keyboard?"

I was so excited to be on the team that I didn't even think about what I was saying as I said, "Yes!" So, I later showed up and realized then I was just going to be playing with my left hand, and as piano players know, the left hand is harder, and somehow playing with only my left hand seemed harder than using both hands! There I was, just playing the bass parts one-handed. And I don't know how they let me play as long as I did. It was quite a few months until finally someone said, "I don't think we need the bass part anymore!"

But during those months, every worship set was going by so fast that I didn't have enough time to think through the one single note I needed to play at a time. I was thinking, $C \ldots G \ldots C \ldots G$, and somehow messing just that up. I definitely didn't have the capacity or the bandwidth to think about asking God what He wanted to say or responding to Him.

As time went on, however, I had more opportunities to play and sing. I continued practicing on my own and on other worship teams. As my skill grew, I was freed up in my mind to engage my own heart in worship, and then finally I had the capacity to engage the Holy Spirit and dialogue with Him during the set.

Receive

Once you ask, then you position your heart to listen and receive. Believe God loves to speak and then continue to lead with strength and courage. It's very important not to strive in the waiting. There is nothing you can do to make God speak. So, continue to worship and lead the people into His presence.

During our worship sets at Radiant Church, we always plan to create space somewhere in the set, even if it's only a short moment within worship, to wait on the Holy Spirit. As a team, we all activate this idea of active listening. We all wait, and often someone on our team will feel a melody, a theme, a rhythm, an idea, or even a chorus. They boldly play out or sing out what they feel or hear, and the rest of the team joins by participating on their instrument or waiting for an appropriate place to jump in vocally.

Is It on a Theme?

Sometimes, during a set, I will immediately get a sense of what God is wanting to speak to us. I will feel the theme of hope or peace in my preparation time during the week, during rehearsal, or even as the set begins. Sometimes, on the other hand, I haven't had a real sense until the musicians begin to play during an instrumental, and suddenly, the prophetic spirit is released by the musicians. The Holy Spirit then highlights a theme to me. I can sing out this theme and create a prophetic song about the theme as the Spirit leads. Hope, joy, the goodness of God, His faithfulness, or peace are themes He is often speaking to us.

Is It on a Melody or Rhythm?

As singers, we cannot forget about the prophetic musicians and the integral role they play on our team. We will talk about the prophetic musicians in greater detail in chapter 9, but regarding the prophetic song, oftentimes the prophetic musician is the one who brings in a new melody, progression, or rhythm, and that brings the anointing. The ministry of the Holy Spirit happens through what they are playing on their instrument. Seasoned prophetic singers can recognize the part that is being highlighted and do one of a few things.

Prophetic singers can be still and let the power of the prophetic music minister to hearts in the room. Sometimes, this is all that is needed from the worship team. I've been on many sets where the musicians carried the prophetic spirit. The musicians would play and prophesy on their instruments. The anointing would flow, and the word of the Lord would go forth through the music. During these times, no words are needed. Sometimes, words can get in the way. The Lord just wants to go straight to our hearts at such times. He uses words to speak to us, but He also loves to transcend verbal language and speak directly to our souls.

Have you ever been in a worship set and nothing is sung, but you begin to feel your mood change, or maybe you feel a breakthrough in your soul during the music, a shift in the atmosphere in the room, or even a shift in your own soul? It can feel like hope seeping in out of nowhere or can be the tangible presence of God.

One of my favorite drummers will play in a worship service, and oftentimes, breakthrough is released in the room when he plays. The band will be doing an instrumental moment, and he will just begin to play with more unction as the spirit of prophecy comes on him. I mean, you can watch the room break open as he plays.

I have to brag on my husband, Caleb, for a moment. He is an anointed prophetic musician. When he plays the piano, beautiful melodies come out of him. He has spent years and years in these prophetic worship environments and has learned how to hear the voice of God and play a melody that unlocks the heart of the people to hear what the voice of God is saying corporately. As singers, we must discern when and if words are necessary.

Prophetic singers can have a melody or rhythm come to mind. You can lean into that part and let the Holy Spirit tell you what to sing in correlation with where the music is going. Maybe the electric guitar is playing a melody like 1, 4, 6, 3, 1, and the melody is highlighted. Instead of creating your own melody for your prophetic song, you could join forces with the established melody and sing your first couple lines to the melody, or potentially even your chorus. This partnership between musician and proclaimer is seen throughout the Scriptures!

The audiobook version contains three examples of this: an example of a prophetic instrumental moment, an example of a prophetic song that is started with a melody from a musician, and an example of a prophetic song that is started with a rhythm from a musician.

Release

Once you step off the cliff and begin to sing out, commit to your cliff jump. Don't trail off or abruptly stop. Sing to be heard! If you go for it, really go for it! Muster up boldness and confidence and let it rip! You develop boldness and confidence the more you step out and try it. Just like most things, confidence comes from repetition and rehearsing. Once you take the deep dive into singing out, make sure you follow through and continue to sing loudly enough to be heard and clearly enough to be understood.

Let the melody and feel of your singing fit with the words you are singing. Use musical dynamics like crescendo, decrescendo, loud, soft, build, or crash out to develop the song. Lead your musicians to follow you with these dynamic cues. They will lean into their prophetic gifting and play with you, but cues are helpful so that you flow together. If I am building and getting louder and louder and then suddenly want to bring it down and sing something sweetly, I can cue the team.

Stay on theme, as you let the Holy Spirit lead. Rely on your history of hearing the voice of God and your history in developing biblical language to give you the right words to say.

Be a student of the room and know if you are bringing others with you into the moment. If you are on minute eight of a prophetic song about your struggle and how you wish your brother would quit teasing you, and you look out and the room is standing awkwardly wishing they could sneak out of the room, it's time to wrap it up and move on to a corporate worship song!

If you look out and the room is responding to the song, allow the ministry of the Holy Spirit to work in their hearts. Give Him space to do this.

Something we say to our worship leaders and our teams all the time is: If it's not there, don't force it. What we mean by this is it is important that we don't sing something randomly in the hope it goes somewhere. We want to be releasing what God is doing and saying in the room. So, there is no need to fill space just to fill space. It's much better at that moment to go back into corporate worship. But if He speaks, lean in even to the whisper.

The Chorus

Remember the prophetic song of Moses and Miriam from chapter 3? Miriam closed out the time of worship by singing a chorus. This is a great way to end your prophetic song. There is no formula though, so it's not necessary, but it is a simple way to bring the room back into unity through singing the theme of your prophetic song.

Choose a phrase or idea that encompasses the theme of your song. Repeat this phrase over and over again. Invite the room to engage in singing this with you. Choruses bring unity and allow the room to sing with their own voices and echo what you sang out in your song.

Rest

Releasing a prophetic song can feel vulnerable and exposing. Once you complete your song, it's important to rest in your identity as a son or daughter of God. Go back to the shadow of His wing and let Him hide you as you rest and receive His peace. It is not the time to critique what you sang or come up with ways you could have done better. Just rest in your identity as His child.

You opened yourself up to release a song. In doing so, you experienced a vulnerableness associated with that. I have experienced firsthand the backlash, mental traffic, and lies directly following my obedience to sing out a prophetic song. It's only after these times that I have made an impulsive or a reactionary vow to never sing again! The enemy wants to come in during these moments of vulnerability and sow doubt in your heart about your natural abilities as a singer, musician, or leader. The adversary wants you to doubt your ability to hear God and your ability to prophesy. I have experienced mental traffic where my stream of consciousness goes away from worship and sounds something like this: *That was the worst. I am never stepping out and prophesying in worship again. In fact, I'm done. Yep, I had a nice run, but it's over. I am quitting. I don't even know what I sang. Was it even biblical? Ugh! And my pastor was in the front row. No one looked like they had any clue what I was saying. My team hates me. I have been wasting my time as a worship leader. I give up.* Though thoughts like these are normal, they can cause you to draw away and isolate. That's why it's a crucial part of the rest phase to debrief as a team.

Debrief

It's important to surround yourself in truth afterward. Surround yourself with encouraging voices. After worship sets, our teams do a quick debrief. Our debriefings serve a few purposes:

1. **To uplift and encourage each other.** The debrief is not the time to bring critiques. I like to come with one or two encouragements for my team, specific things I can say to encourage a team member: "Hey, Johnny, I loved that spontaneous melody you played in between song two and three. It was so beautiful and ushered us right into the next song. Sandy, you crushed that harmony part on the bridge of 'Let it Rain.' So fire!" It's also important to give encouragement to the entire team: "Thanks for the way you all leaned into that spontaneous moment. It felt like everyone was listening to each other and going in the same

direction. It's such a blast being on this team together!" We want to combat the natural tendency to self-deprecate after we play and sing by bringing truth and life through our words after each set. If this is awkward for you, I encourage you to begin practicing this anyway. It's only awkward because you haven't done it much. And let me tell you, your team will be thankful for your words of encouragement. Every team member should be contributing affirming words from time to time to build unity and to create this positive culture of holding each other up.

2. **To highlight any points of confusion or places in the set that needed clarity.** For example, during the second song, maybe we missed the cue to go back into the chorus. How can we catch the cue and stay together next time? Maybe we open our eyes and give a verbal cue instead of a hand signal? This is not the time, however, to highlight the mistakes of individual team members. This is simply a time to regroup and find a solution or way forward for our next set.

3. **To celebrate.** We want to take joy and celebrate what we did together. We exalted Jesus and led our congregation the best we could into His presence. That's something to celebrate!

Short, simple, and uplifting debriefings help us stay unified with positive attitudes, filled with truth, and then we are guided by that truth. These times will combat the mental traffic and lies we face after sets.

Prophetic Songs in a Corporate Context

In corporate worship, especially during our Sunday morning services, it is important to remember our main goal or top priority is to lead the people of God into a place of worship and encounter. Our prophetic songs will reflect that. If we spend seven minutes out of our twenty minutes singing our own spontaneous, made-up song, we will lose room engagement. As we discussed before, one way to bring unity to the room around the prophetic song is to end your song in a chorus. The people in the room will be listening as you prophesy in song, but to help them engage on a deeper level, find a phrase or sentence that encompasses the main idea of the prophetic song and repeat it over and over again. Sometimes, I will give a verbal cue and say something like, "Let's all sing this chorus together," to help the room see we have transitioned from singing our own songs to singing corporately. The room will begin to sing this chorus with me, and we will have corporate agreement and rallying behind the prophetic song that was released.

Prophetic Songs Do Not Have to Be Spontaneous

This is one of the greatest misconceptions about the prophetic song. Prophetic is not synonymous with spontaneous. Often, the two words correlate, but a prophetic song by rule is not always spontaneous. A prophetic song is prophetic because it reveals what the Lord is saying, not because you came up with it on the fly during worship. Some prophetic singers rehearse singing around a theme that they feel the Lord is highlighting for a particular set. Others will write down word for word exactly what they want to sing.

Many times, as I pray during the week and invite the Holy Spirit to share with me what is on the heart of the Father for a particular service, or worship and prayer set, I receive insight or a nudge in a certain direction. Sometimes, I will take that idea and sit down at the piano or with my journal and begin to sing and write about the topic.

I remember one Saturday night service when the Lord clearly impressed on my heart a prophetic song I had sung straight to His heart months previously in private during one of my times with Him. I had sung out the theme and main ideas of that moment in the secret place with the Father. That Saturday night, He asked me to sing the prophetic song in the room in the service. I had not planned for this. The song was not a spontaneous one, as I had sung this idea in my home in a puddle of tears weeks before when I was alone with the Father. As I sang it on Saturday night at church, the idea I had sung about months ago developed further into this beautiful song. The entirety of this prophetic song can be heard on the audiobook:

He is closer than we know and nearer than we realize
Some of you have felt like you are on a boat and the boat has holes.
And there is a storm, and you feel like you're sinking.
But let me tell you where Jesus is. He's in your boat.
He's in your boat, and it won't sink 'cause He is in the boat.
And let me tell you something. He is calming the storm, and He is calming your soul.
He is in the boat right with you! He is right with you. He's right with you. He is in the boat.
Do not fear, do not fear, He's right here.
He's right here. And right now, He's ministering to your soul.
He is in the boat with you, and it's not sinking. He is calming the storm.
YOU ARE NOT ALONE!

In just one to two weeks, the initial pandemic shutdown happened. I went into our archives and played back this prophetic song for my own soul many times in the weeks that followed. It was a song of hope that God released through me before we even knew we would be in the crisis that came a few weeks later.

My Own Personal Testimony

I have had times in a worship service where a singer has begun to sing from the Lord's perspective, and I have been sure that they were singing straight to me. Some of these moments have altered and changed my life. I have heard the Lord's voice through prophetic songs. I still remember one prophetic song that moved me and encouraged me during a season of life when I felt stuck and hopeless.

I had been doing the same old thing day after day. God felt distant, and though I loved Him, I didn't feel His nearness. My love was growing cold. It was during this time that I was in a worship service when a singer began to sing a prophetic song from the Lord's perspective. She sang these words: *"It's been hard, harder than you thought to get to know Me, to come and find Me. But it has not been wasted time; it has not been wasted hours. I promise it will be worth it. I promise you will know Me.*

'Cause this is who you are: you are My friend." Her song ended with this simple yet profound chorus: *"Reach again for Me!"*

It was as if Jesus were singing straight to me, "Rachel, would you reach for Me again? Would you say *yes* again to the pursuit of My heart?"

The power in the singer's phrases connected with melody and the prophetic, anointed musicians hit my heart, and I wept under the power of the Holy Spirit ministering to me in that moment. This prophetic encouragement pulled me out of that dreary, monotonous hopelessness I was feeling and moved me to rise up in my pursuit of Jesus. I decided that day that I was going to reach again for the Lord.

The girl who sang out this spontaneous song sang it in a room full of people with thousands more viewing online. But it was ministering to me personally, and I could see many others being touched by the Holy Spirit as she sang out what the Father was saying to His children.

Closing Prayer

Pray this with me. It may help to read it aloud.

Jesus,
Thank You for the partnership You desire with us. Thank You for the Holy Spirit and the gift of prophecy. Would You anoint us to prophesy? Give us the gift of prophecy. As we activate this gift, would You anoint the songs? Would You speak to us what You are desiring to say to Your people? Give the prophetic singers courage and boldness to step out in faith to release the songs. Thank You that You are always speaking to Your people. Grant us ears to hear what Your Spirit is saying and the boldness and courage to declare it.
    Amen.

Prompt

I would like to give you some space to practice prophetic singing! It's wonderful to read about it, but to really activate it in your life, you need to practice doing it.

Take your prompt from chapter 4 on developing biblical language and choose either Psalm 23 or 27. If you have the audiobook, directly following this chapter, we have added three live band chord progressions to help you. If not, and you play an instrument, play a simple chord progression and begin singing to the Lord using phrases from your chosen psalm. Singing acapella is always an option as well.

Sing the verse.

Then sing some of the phrases you wrote down.

Maybe new phrases or ideas will come to you. Sing those out as well.

Is there one phrase that encompasses the main idea? Or one melody hook that you keep coming back to? Use those to create a chorus and repeat your chorus over and over again!

This time, choose a theme like one of the fruits of the Spirit—love, joy, peace, patience, kindness, goodness, faithfulness, gentleness, or self-control. Choose which perspective you will sing from: God's voice to us, your voice to God, or a declaration of truth. Practice singing phrases and scriptures that connect to this theme.

Lastly, find a melody. Then create a chorus using that melody that states the main idea of your song.

A Testimony

One of my most favorite and meaningful times in worship happened during my church's yearly worship and creative conference. I had the opportunity to play electric guitar for this particular set, and I remember being focused on the band and what was happening musically, but I heard some very impactful words during a prophetic song one of the singers sang: "You didn't waste your time." I went back later and listened over and over again to this song as the words ministered to me and the season I was in.

During this time in my life, I was struggling with a couple lies that I was behind where I should be in life and I needed to do more, produce more, and have more to show. The Lord had asked me a year before to be obedient and simplify my life. He asked me to put career and other life goals on hold to focus on my relationship with Him.

So, when I heard this prophetic song that spoke all about history with the Father and the time that seemed useless or a waste was in fact God ordained, I realized I wasn't behind but actually right on time. It was necessary for my history with Him. That chorus spoke directly into that season of saying yes to the Lord and giving Him my time and my life. It wasn't a waste!

—Tom

Partnership: Prophetic Singing and the Prophetic Musician

"Praise the Lord! Praise God in His sanctuary; praise Him in His mighty firmament! Praise Him for His mighty acts; praise Him according to His excellent greatness! Praise Him with the sound of the trumpet; praise Him with the lute and harp! Praise Him with the timbrel and dance; praise Him with stringed instruments and flutes! Praise Him with loud cymbals; praise Him with clashing cymbals! Let everything that has breath praise the Lord. Praise the Lord!" (Psalm 150:1–6 NKJV)

We have spent most of this book highlighting the role and calling of the prophetic singer. This chapter will address the role of the prophetic musician and the unity and power that comes when the singer and musician team together in the power of the Holy Spirit. You just may discover you identify more as a musician than as a singer as you read this chapter.

There are glimpses of prophetic musicians scattered throughout Scripture, and some of the greatest prophetic declarations came forth because the musicians first prophesied on their instrument before the prophetic word or declaration was made. Let's look specifically at this dynamic.

The Power of Music

Many times, music will open the door for the prophetic spirit to flow. We don't need music to prophesy, but music can usher in the prophetic spirit in a powerful way. We have all had similar experiences listening to music. Let me describe a few scenarios.

Scenario 1

You are in college. You had a great day in class. You aced your test and had fun with friends, and you got home and went straight to your room to put on your favorite emo band. After a few songs, you begin to feel. You mellow out, and slowly a surprising sadness washes over you. Your circumstances say you should feel great. You received a great grade on your test, and you had fun throughout the day. But the music speaks something else to you. The music unlocks your heart to feel an emotion. Now you are sitting in bed, feeling the weight of the world on your shoulders, and you don't know how you can possibly do your homework and your chores while feeling this way. You mope around for the next few hours with a negative attitude and go to bed feeling depressed.

> **We don't need music to prophesy, but music can usher in the prophetic spirit in a powerful way.**

Scenario 2

The morning was full of chaos and confusion. Your family made you late for church again, and you are annoyed by the way no one else seemed to care that they were going to be late. As you drive, you remember the work project you are behind in and how stressful work is lately. You have been feeling frustrated and stressed. You just can't seem to catch a break. Even your homelife is not as it should be. Discouragement sets in like a thick fog as you pull into the church parking lot. "Late again," you mutter to yourself as you put your car in park and walk from the furthest parking space toward the church building.

You find your seat inside, and worship has already begun. Within minutes, your heart begins to open, and as the worship songs are playing, your soul starts to reset. You come into alignment with truth. You take your eyes off your problems and look straight at Jesus. You leave church feeling refreshed and ready to lean into the grace of God over your life to tackle the upcoming week.

Both of these scenarios support and strengthen the idea that music is powerful. Music can make us feel both positive and negative emotions. Music can prey on our emotions. It can also unlock our hearts and make us sensitive to receive. Will we receive messages of hope or of despair?

In the first scenario, the teenager's heart was unlocked by the music to receive the message of sadness and negativity. The message could have been communicated by the lyrics of the song, the feel of the music, and maybe even the spirit in which the song was created. In the second scenario, the person was already distraught and feeling down. As the music played, the discouraged soul found hope again. The music opened him up so he could receive the message.

Music is a powerful tool that can unlock the human heart and cause it to open and receive. Let's look at the ones who create music.

The Prophetic Musician

Just as described in an earlier chapter, a prophetic singer is someone who prophesies using melody and words. Similarly, a prophetic musician is someone who prophesies on their instrument. A musician plays their instrument. A *prophetic* musician listens to the Holy Spirit and leans into his prophetic anointing as he plays his instrument.

The story in 1 Samuel 16:14–23 displays this beautifully:

> *Now the Spirit of the Lord departed from Saul, and a harmful spirit from the Lord tormented him. And Saul's servants said to him, "Behold now, a harmful spirit from God is tormenting you. Let our lord now command your servants who are before you to seek out a man who is skillful in playing the lyre, and when the harmful spirit from God is upon you, he will play it, and you will be well." So Saul said to his servants, "Provide for me a man who can play well and bring him to me." One of the young men answered,* **"Behold, I have seen a son of Jesse the Bethlehemite, who is skillful in playing, a man of valor, a man of war, prudent in speech, and a man of good presence, and the Lord is with him."** *Therefore Saul sent messengers to Jesse and said, "Send me David your son, who is with the sheep." And Jesse took a donkey laden with bread and a skin of wine and a young goat and sent them by David his son to Saul. And David came to Saul and entered his service. And Saul loved him greatly, and he became his armor-bearer. And Saul sent to Jesse, saying, "Let David remain in my service, for he has found favor in my sight." And whenever the harmful spirit from God was upon Saul,* **David took the lyre and played it with his hand. So Saul was refreshed and was well, and the harmful spirit departed from him.** *(ESV)*

Saul was in distress. His soul was struggling and desperate for reprieve. The servants recommended a young man who was not only a skilled musician but a musician who was filled with the spirit of God to play for the king. The servant knew David not only to be skilled, but someone who the Lord was with. Just two verses before our story began, we read in 1 Samuel 16 that God had anointed David to be the next King of Israel, and when Samuel the prophet anointed him, the scripture says, *"From that day on the Spirit of the Lord came powerfully upon David"* (v. 13).

I am guessing when David was called to come and play before Saul that he wasn't playing the famous pop song he heard the local band play the week before. I doubt he randomly selected a song he knew. More than likely, David leaned into the Spirit of God that was upon him and played out of that place. Maybe it was a song he grew up knowing, maybe he wrote the song, or maybe it was just a combination of melody and rhythms he was penning spontaneously as he played. The point is David played out of a place of relationship with God, and it ministered to the heart and soul of Saul until the distressing spirit left him. What if David wrote, *"The Lord is my shepherd, I shall not want. He makes me lie down in green pastures,"* as a prophetic song over King Saul in his distress?

First, David cultivated his talent and skill unseen by man for years in hiddenness. Then, the Spirit of God came upon David, and he played his instrument before King Saul and the distressing spirit left.

I have gotten the opportunity to lead with some incredible musicians over the past fifteen years, and their musicianship is excellent. I have watched these musicians grow in their skills as musicians. For years, they have played onstage for two hours, six days a week; and on top of that, they have attended weekly rehearsals while finding time to practice at home on their own. They put in serious time to be better musicians. As the years have gone by, they stand out as some of the leading musicians in worship ministry. But one thing that shines forth more than that is the spirit of prophecy that falls when they play their instruments.

You have to understand that, during those long hours playing every day, they did more than just become better musicians. They engaged with the Holy Spirit. They asked Him to fill them. They asked for melodies from heaven. They started prophesying on their instruments, not just playing them. During those decades, they were cultivating their life in God and growing in relationship with Jesus. Many on our Radiant Church worship team are examples of prophetic musicians; they don't just play their instrument skillfully, but they engage with the Holy Spirit on and off the stage so that, when they play, something happens in the Spirit.

The Power of Unity

I want to share with you my all-time favorite example from the Bible of the unity and power of prophetic musicians and singers. In 1 Samuel

9–10, the prophet Samuel went to anoint the first king of Israel. The people had demanded a king, and God answered them by choosing Saul to be that king. The prophet Samuel anointed Saul to be the first king of Israel and then spoke these prophetic words to Saul:

> *After that you shall come to the hill of God where the Philistine garrison is. And it will happen, when you have come there to the city, that you will meet a group of prophets coming down from the high place with a stringed instrument, a tambourine, a flute, and a harp before them; and they will be prophesying. Then the Spirit of the Lord will come upon you, and you will prophesy with them and be turned into another man. And let it be, when these signs come to you, that you do as the occasion demands; for God is with you. (1 Samuel 10:5–7 NKJV)*

A few verses later, we read that, *"When [Saul] and his servant arrived at Gibeah, a procession of prophets met him; the Spirit of God came powerfully upon him, and he joined in their prophesying"* (v. 10). So, what Samuel had prophesied came to pass.

Let me dive into these verses with you for a minute. We have a group of prophets, and at least four of them were prophetic musicians. One was playing a stringed instrument, another a tambourine, a flute, and a harp. As they played, they began to prophesy. Let me put this in modern-day terms for you. This was a prophetic worship team! They were a four-piece band, leaving the high place where they had been worshipping, singing, prophesying, and playing their instruments before God. Saul met up with the prophetic worship team as they were continuing to play and prophesy on their way down from the hill of the Lord. When Saul joined them, the Spirit of God came upon him, and he began to prophesy, too!

Here it is! It's such a good picture of what we want to do within our worship teams. We want unity. We want the musicians and the ones on microphones engaging with the Spirit. The spirit of prophecy can begin to flow as the team unifies. The four-piece band from 1 Samuel 10 was unified. The singers were joining the same prophetic spirit that the band was operating under, and the prophetic message and word were delivered.

Cultivating Unity between the Musician and Singer

Unity doesn't just happen because everyone played the right chord and hit the right note at the same time. Unity is something that is cultivated. We do this by developing trust and operating in humility with our team, singers, and musicians alike. As worship teams, we need to be creating a culture where we are listening to one another, preferring one another, and playing as one.

From the Perspective of a Singer

Cultivating *trust* within your team is important. I trust the musicians. This first point is huge! If I get this wrong, I will miss out completely on the power of unity and prophesying together. I trust my musicians that they are pressing in and leaning into what the Spirit is doing and saying. I know our musicians have taken time to develop their personal relationships with Jesus. I know they hear from God! I trust their musicianship. I trust that, as they play, they are listening to the Spirit. I trust they are asking the same questions I am asking, "Holy Spirit, what are You saying? Holy Spirit, where do You want to take this moment?" Then I trust that what they play is going to usher us right into that moment of breakthrough.

> **These times are some of my favorite moments because the Holy Spirit speaks straight to the hearts of individuals in the room, and the music speaks words that no singer could communicate. The music cuts straight to hearts and ministers to the room in a powerful and personal way.**

Another aspect of trust is trusting the musicians will come around you as you take the leap of faith and begin singing spontaneously. Our musicians at Radiant Church are incredible at this.

It is also important to be a team player and walk in humility. I think sometimes as singers we get tripped up by thinking we brought the prophetic song on our own. We are unaware of the table that has been set for us by the prophetic musicians. In our pride or ignorance, we don't realize it was the music that brought the Holy Spirit inspiration.

Elisha, in Judges, called on the musician to come and play so that he could prophesy. Elisha recognized the role of the musicians and the power that comes when they play. I must recognize, like Elisha, the power and significance of the prophetic musician.

I have been in many worship settings when a musician begins to play and operate in the prophetic. The atmosphere in the room changes, and a breakthrough comes. Some of those times, no singer sang out a prophetic song. No words were used to declare. The instruments alone prophesied, and the anointing and breakthrough were released. These times are some of my favorite moments because the Holy Spirit speaks straight to the hearts of individuals in the room, and the music speaks words that no singer could communicate. The music cuts straight to hearts and ministers to the room in a powerful and personal way.

As we begin to step out into something new during worship, whether it be an unscripted worship moment or an instrumental moment, the first thing I do as a singer is listen. We have already talked about listening to the Holy Spirit and operating in the prophetic spirit in a previous chapter, so I simply want to highlight the practical side here. I listen to the musicians. I listen for melodies or rhythms that begin to stand out or have life on them. I listen to the chord progression to hear where the music is going. *Does the progression have a minor or major feel? What is the general feeling the music is portraying?* I listen to the drummer and percussive instruments. *Are we musically building? Are we swelling? Is the music waiting, or are we building into something?* Almost every time I begin to sing, I have grabbed ahold of a melody, a musical feel, or at least one aspect of the music that has already been established by the team, and I use that to launch into the spontaneous prophetic song.

From the Perspective of a Musician

I am always aiming to be tuned into prophetic seasons and the Holy Spirit's thoughts and intentions. Prayer leaders and prophetic singers often are, but it seems musicians don't always recognize this as part of their calling or job description. Tuning into the "things above" as a musician seems to naturally promote unity with prophetic singers who are also tuned in. I am always wanting to create coherence between words and music. I want to find the sweet spot where the music gives the emotional language for the heart to feel and engage with the truths that are being uttered by the Spirit, singers, and prayer leaders.

Practically, I try to always be present, sensitive, and listening to everyone. We all give each other little cues and unique ingredients to what the Spirit is saying or doing.

Sometimes, the music initiates, and other times, a singer does, so I want to cultivate humility and awareness in myself so when a singer or other musician leads off prophetically, I can "honor the point" and endorse the word with supplementing parts for a fuller decree.

Lastly, I recognize it is important for my heart to be free of criticism and resentment toward leaders, singers, and musicians so I can perceive spiritual movement through others with greater clarity, being able to engage and celebrate what's happening.

A lot of times in prophetic environments, all the musicians will "fish" for melodies at the same time. It takes humility to see God moving on other bandmates and to choose to honor the point, allowing them to lead a moment. It's my time to play a supportive roll. The same thing goes when a vocalist is leading a moment. It's important to always be asking what is needed in a moment. Humility as a prophetic musician looks like seeing God moving on the other musicians and singers and serving the moment by supporting it. This can look like playing a countermelody, harmony, or an atmospheric presence, or even not playing at all.

The Spirit Came upon Them

One thing I can't help but notice in these two biblical examples of prophetic musicians is the way the Bible says that the Spirit of God came upon Saul and David and then they prophesied. The Old Testament mentions a handful of times when the Spirit of God came upon a person for a time to do a specific work or to declare a specific word. For example, we read in Judges 3:10, *"The Spirit of the Lord came upon [Othniel] and he judged Israel."* This is also seen in the story I just mentioned about Saul in 1 Samuel 10:10. *"When they came there to the hill, there was a group of prophets to meet him; then the Spirit of God came upon him (Saul), and he prophesied among them* (1 Samuel 10:10). Here are a few more because I love the way God did this with His leaders!

> *But the Spirit of the Lord came upon Gideon; then he blew the trumpet, and the Abiezrites gathered behind him. (Judges 6:34)*

> *And the Spirit of the Lord came mightily upon [Samson], and he tore the lion apart as one would have torn apart a young goat, though he had nothing in his hand. But he did not tell his father or his mother what he had done. (Judges 14:6)*

> *When he came to Lehi, the Philistines came shouting against him. Then the Spirit of the Lord came mightily upon him; and the ropes that were on his arms became like flax that is burned with fire, and his bonds broke loose from his hands. He found a fresh jawbone of a donkey, reached out his hand and took it, and killed a thousand men with it. (Judges 15:14–15)*

Calling all Creatives

This last example is a shout out to all the creatives, tradesmen, and artisans who may not be musicians and singers. This story is for you!

> *Then the Lord spoke to Moses, saying: "See, I have called by name Bezaleel the son of Uri, the son of Hur, of the tribe of Judah. And I have filled him with the Spirit of God, in wisdom, in understanding, in knowledge, and in all manner of workmanship, to design artistic works in gold, in silver, in bronze, in cutting jewels for setting, in carving wood, and to work in all manner of workmanship." (Exodus 31:1–5 NKJV)*

> *And Moses said to the children of Israel, "See, the Lord has called by name Bezalel the son of Uri, the son of Hur, of the tribe of Judah; and He has filled him with the Spirit of God, in wisdom and understanding, in knowledge and all manner of workmanship, to design artistic works, to work in gold and silver and bronze, in cutting jewels for setting, in carving wood, and to work in all manner of artistic workmanship. "And He has put in his heart the ability to teach, in him and Aholiab the son of Ahisamach, of the tribe of Dan. He has filled them with skill to do all manner of work of the engraver and the designer and the tapestry maker, in blue, purple, and scarlet thread, and fine linen, and of the weaver—those who do every work and those who design artistic works. And Bezaleel and Aholiab, and every gifted artisan in whom the Lord has put wisdom and understanding, to know how to do all manner of work for the service of the sanctuary, shall do according to all that the Lord has commanded." (Exodus 35:30–36:1 NKJV)*

Bezaleel was the man God raised up as a master craftsman to create and build the tabernacle of Moses. God gave Moses the pattern for the tabernacle up on the mountain. He instructed Moses to have the tabernacle built. Then He raised up Bezaleel, filled him with the Spirit of God to craft the tabernacle after a pattern, not a blueprint. So here we have again, God filling a man with His Spirit to perform a work. This example is extremely powerful because it speaks to the partnership of God with man as well. God could have just spoken the tabernacle into existence, bypassing the need to have humans, who tend to mess things up. Or, God could have just handed Moses the blueprints for the tabernacle and said, "Here, give this to my guy, Bezaleel. I filled him with My Spirit to follow directions well. He will brainlessly just build exactly what I have asked for without engaging his mind, his creativity, or the gifts that I have put inside him. He will build the tabernacle."

No! That is not our God. He chose to partner with man to see His will and purposes on the earth be fulfilled. He gifted Bezaleel with talent, talent that Bezaleel stewarded for years. There were probably decades of honing his craft and growing in his skills as an artisan, using his creativity to plan, design, and build beautiful things. Then God filled him with His Spirit. Bezaleel, with his skills and talent, partnered with the Spirit of God and used the pattern God gave Moses to build a beautiful, creative, and innovative tabernacle. This is exactly how God wants to use us.

We now have the indwelling Holy Spirit who lives inside us. When we are born again and receive Jesus, He comes and makes His home in us. We can still receive power from the Holy Spirit, and we still ask to be filled with the Spirit, but we always have the indwelling Spirit and access to Him. Singers, musicians, artisans, and every follower of Jesus always have access to the indwelling Holy Spirit. This means our ability to communicate with the Spirit and grow in our relationship with Him is not hindered by outside circumstances. We can be used to prophesy. We can ask Him to speak anytime! We can partner with the Holy Spirit and create beautiful things. We can skillfully use our craft for the glory of God.

Closing Prayer

Pray this with me. It may help to read it aloud.

Father,
We thank You for the role of the prophetic musician throughout Scripture and the role of the prophetic musicians today. Thank You for the way you have created us to partner with Your heart and join You in declaring Your Word to the nations and individuals.

I ask that You raise up prophetic musicians in this hour. Anoint ones who are in love with Jesus, skilled on their instruments, and operating in the power of the Holy Spirit. I pray You speak identity and calling over the musicians lost in music with no meaning or purpose. I pray You reach the musicians jaded by church as usual. I ask that our musicians in churches across America and the world would be struck with the high calling to play their instrument before the Lord. Call them into leadership and into identity, that they would have a prophetic spirit and prophesy the Word of the Lord to their generation.

I pray for unity among band members and worship teams and unity between the prophetic singers and prophetic musicians. Thank You for the role of the prophetic musician. Call musicians out and raise them up as holy unto the Lord.

Amen.

Prompt

Listen to music! If you have the audiobook, I have included two different live instrumental worship moments at the end of this chapter from our team at Radiant City Music.

You may also listen to an instrumental worship album.

Listen to the first worship moment. As you listen, pull out your journal or write in the space provided below. Ask the Lord to speak to you through the music. Unless you feel prompted to do so, don't feel pressured to sing in these moments. Just listen and let the prophetic musicians minister to you. Journal as the Lord speaks to you.

Do the same thing for the second instrumental worship moment.

A Testimony

For most of my life I have moved from place to place, sometimes moving every few months. It was exhausting. My dream in life was to settle down and be a place of safety for other people. I have always said yes to where I felt I was supposed to go because I trusted that one day the Lord would give me a place to call home.

During a prayer meeting at the church I had been attending for a few months, one of the singers began singing a prophetic song about Mary of Bethany. She sang about breaking open our vials upon Jesus' feet and filling the room with our fragrance of praise. While this was all happening, I kept hearing the Father say over me, "My sweet daughter, it's time. It's time for you to stay. Stay and be like Mary. Stay and put down roots and pour out your jar. Stay and be Mary." In all my years of serving and obedience with the Father, I had never heard Him ask me to stay somewhere. It was an answer to prayers I have been praying for years. And He answered in a moment during this prophetic song.

Fast forward two years, and I am still serving at the same church and getting married in just a few months. I have put roots down and have found deep friendships and community. My dream and my desires that I have been longing for and praying for are becoming reality. And I will never forget that one worship and prayer meeting when the Lord spoke straight to me through a prophetic song and whispered to my heart, "Stay."

—Gretta

Singing on a Worship Team

I love practicals, and I love the details. I love steps, lists, and timelines, and I read every word of an instruction manual before attempting to build anything. That's just how I am wired. I am not your typical creative mind. I couldn't bring myself to give you a resource without including a chapter simply on the basic mechanics of singing. Welcome to chapter 10, my own *Singing for Dummies* in a worship context.

Excellence and Stewardship

Everyone can sing, as I've said from the very beginning, and almost everyone can become a better singer. If you aren't tone deaf, you can become a better singer. This should be encouraging for the average singer, knowing it's possible to grow and get better. This should also be encouraging and challenging to the singers who have been singing for a while. The ceiling you feel over your singing isn't permanent if you diligently work on it. What if singers in the church began to hone their craft like singers in musical theater or singers taking stages in secular arenas? Stewardship of our singing gift requires us to grow our skill and become excellent singers, not just anointed singers.

The Basics

Just breathe—but do it correctly! Correct breathing gets massively overlooked in most contemporary worship circles. Our worship songs allow us the space in between lines and even words to breathe wherever we want to. We end up singing songs like this Radiant City Music chorus of "From this House" with numerous unnecessary breaths.

> "From this house **(inhale)** be lifted up, **(inhale)** From this heart **(inhale)** let praise pour forth, **(inhale)** Our hosanna **(inhale)** belongs to You, **(inhale)** We won't withhold the **(inhale)** praise you're due."

Imagine if I were speaking those same words out loud instead of singing them. Imagine if I breathed at the same places. For fun, take a moment and say this chorus aloud, but inhale at the spaces I have indicated above. It's a ridiculous amount of inhaling, and it is physically unnecessary to breathe that much. We never want to breathe in the middle of a sentence and certainly not in the middle of a thought or word whenever possible. This breathing problem is usually seen in singers who have soft, aspirated onsets for style purposes or weak breath control.

Breathe at the end of phrases, where there are commas or periods. You want your breaths to be silent; inhale in through your mouth and exhale again out of the mouth.

Breathe from Your Diaphragm

We all know we are supposed to breathe from our diaphragm when we sing. Someone at one point told us that. But who really does it? Who really knows how to do it? A breath from your diaphragm better supports your sound. Here is a simple exercise you can do to help you take breaths from the correct place.

Lay flat on your back. Position a heavy book sideways on your tummy. Your hands should be down by your sides. Now, focus on your breathing and inhale in such a way so that the book rises as you inhale. It can take a few minutes to focus on where the breath is coming from. You should be able to have the book rise as you inhale and then fall as you exhale. As you continue to do this for another minute, focus on the mechanics of what your body is doing to breathe this way. Notice where the breath is coming from.

> **Stewardship of our singing gift requires us to grow our skill and become excellent singers, not just anointed singers.**

Now, stand up and try to breathe the same way. If that's not working for you, you can also look in a mirror as you breathe and notice if your chest and/or shoulders are rising and falling instead of your stomach

When I am learning a new song, I chart out my breathing. I will touch on this again in the preparing to sing and rehearsal section. Here is an example of a breathing chart for a song. I add these little breath marks, also called *luftpause*, and practice breathing at appropriate times in the song that make sense and best help the flow of the song. Sometimes, I play around with breathing in different spots to see which one flows better.

New Rain
Caleb Culver | Richard Adolph

V1 ʼWhat is the melody of heaven's song
ʼWhat's been written on the heavenly scroll
For this cityʼ

ʼWhat would it mean to be a city restored
ʼPresence and power like revivals of old
In this cityʼ

CH ʼPrayer in His houseʼ
I can feel the walls are shaking
Praise in the streetʼ
I can hear the city singing
Ohʼ the Lord, the Lord is here

V2 ʼNow is the time for us to seek his face
ʼBreak up the fallow ground with tears and praise
In this cityʼ

ʼAnd like a river let your justice roll ʼ
Streams of healing rushing from your throne
To this city

BR ʼI hear the sound
ʼSee the cloud
On the way

ʼI know it's been dry
ʼHear me now
It's gonna rain

Example of a breathing chart

Posture Is Important

Everyone on the planet needs to hear this. Posture is important! We are a generation of people who refuse to stand up straight. We are all walking around willingly looking like the Hunchback of Notre Dame. Because of this, we have invented contraptions you stick on your back that will vibrate to remind you to fix your posture and straighten up. There are so many reasons your posture matters, but here I will give you a few reasons that correlate with singing.

1. With good posture, you optimize your breathing by giving more space for air to fill your body. With optimized breathing, your voice will sound better.
2. With good posture, you can hold more air in your body which will allow for longer held notes and better breath support.
3. When your body posture is open, your sound will have an open sound. Open sound is a better sound.

Singing Posture

Let's look at proper posture starting with our feet and working our way up the body.

1. Feet—stand hip width apart. You want to think of your feet as tripods. Keep your weight balanced on your feet, using the ball of your foot, your heel, and the bone below your pinkie toe.
2. Legs—keep your legs straight but do not lock your knees.
3. Back—keep it straight!
4. Hands—keep them down by your sides. No crossing your arms. When you cross your arms, you close off some of your sound
5. Shoulders—have them back and lowered, never raised.
6. Head—keep it level. Don't move your head up as you ascend the scale, and don't lower it as you hit lower notes. Keep it loose and still.

Inside Your Mouth Posture and Positioning

On the roof of your mouth, you have your hard palate, and your soft palate is right behind it. You want your soft palate lifted as you sing. As you lift your soft palate, you want to open the back of your throat. You can imagine you have an orange and need to try and fit the orange in the back of your throat. These two positionings will help your sound be open and lifted.

Your tongue has a resting place in your mouth. When you are not needing it to create a sound, the tip of your tongue should rest on the inside of your bottom teeth.

Sing in Key

So much of singing in our modern, contemporary worship services is reliant on our ears. We no longer are reading notated music when we sing worship songs. Our ears are helping us instantaneously find the next note of the song. So, it's important as a singer to develop our musical ear. Here are a few ear training exercises that are a lot of fun to try.

Find a friend and have them play a note on the piano. Immediately sing the note that they played on "la." If you hit the note dead on, your friend will play the next note and again immediately sing that note on "la." If you can't find the note, or you hit a note that is not the intended note, have your friend continue to play the note until your voice matches the note on the piano. This will help you hear if you are on the note but slightly sharp or flat. Work on correcting these errors and decreasing the amount of time it takes you to find each note and sing it correctly.

You can try the next ear training exercise by yourself or with a friend. Play a series of 3 consecutive different notes. Immediately, try to sing the melody that was just played. If this becomes too easy, increase the number of notes played in the melody until it is challenging. The notes don't need to be in the same key to make it even more challenging!

Here is one last ear training exercise for you. It involves hearing intervals. On the piano, play the 1(do) and then try to sing the 3 (mi). Play the 3 and see if the note you sang matches. Play the 1 again and try to sing the 5 (so). Play the 5 and see if your note matches. Continue this exercise using different intervals.

Pitch

Sing the right notes! For some, this is easier said than done. I have heard even the most renown singers hit awful notes on stage that they did not intend to hit. Admit it, you have watched those YouTube singer fails on repeat! I have my fair share of stories where I did not sing the correct note. Beyond just hitting the correct note, within that note, you can hit it sharp or flat. So, watch your pitch.

Diction and Phrasing

Diction includes pronunciation, enunciation, accent, inflection, and intonation. I will lump in phrasing in this section as well. Sing the words as you would say them. Enunciate clearly so the congregation can clearly hear the words you are singing. To sound cool, some singers will sing words with a fake accent or odd intonation that is unnatural. Most of the time, your effort to be cool will backfire, and you will just sound weird or unnatural. Notice the phrasing. Sing phrases in such a way so the lyrics make sense. Don't separate one idea by your phrasing but keep it all together.

Blending

What is blending? When I think of blending, I think of a really good choir. The individual singers that make up a choir have all learned how to blend their voices together. They have surrendered some of their personal style in favor of a more blended sound. Because of this, choirs have a beautifully smooth and whole sound.

Blending is a skill we can learn and grow in, and it definitely has a place on our worship teams. Tone, diction, pronunciation, dynamics, intonation, phrasing, volume, and rhythm are all to be considered when trying to create a blended sound with other singers.

My first piece of advice when trying to grow in blending would be to listen. To blend, one must listen to others. In a choir, all the singers are listening to each other and going after a unified sound so all the voices blend together. In contrast, on our worship teams, we typically do have one leader whose voice will stand out as they lead the congregation. Everyone else on stage should listen and blend with the worship leader as well as with each other.

Take Singing lessons

You can become a better singer if you want to. We want to sing beautifully, and we wish our voices sounded like other people at times. But singers don't always go out and pursue lessons. More often than not, singers who sing on a Sunday do not practice in the way that musicians who play on a Sunday practice. The truth is you have not hit your ceiling, and there is always room for growth. Steward the gift and grow it! Find a vocal teacher or coach in your area. Sometimes, area colleges and universities have professors who also give lessons to the general public, not just college students. Maybe there is a skilled vocal teacher in your church who would be willing to help you develop your voice and singing skill. Learn more about your voice and what you are capable of!

> As the worship leader, it is important to sing in such a way that others can follow you. One of the main goals of music artists, opera singers, Broadway singers, and even local choirs is to sing in such a way that others will want to listen. As a worship leader, your goal is much different. Your goal is to sing in such a way that others will want to worship and sing along with you. You don't want them to be spectators or listeners. You want them to be active participants. So beyond singing confidently, how else can you sing to lead?

Practice More Than Just Your Next Setlist

Practice more than just your next setlist. To grow and get better, it's important that you practice and rehearse songs, warm-ups and vocal exercises that will challenge you. Most of our current contemporary worship songs were written so the entire congregation can sing and engage with the song. This means that our songs were written to be easy to sing. These corporate worship songs are powerful in that they bring the room together with simple songs that everyone can sing. If these are the only songs you practice, you will not get better as a singer. You may get better at singing those songs, but you will not grow in vocal skill.

Find songs that are vocally challenging or highlight one of your vocal weaknesses. Practice these songs! Vocal exercises are another way to grow your skill. These exercises can be key to enhancing your voice, expanding your range, honing your tone, and learning your registers and vocal breaks.

Singer Roles

Let's look at different roles available for singers.

Worship Leader Singing

Confidence, confidence, confidence, and again I say, confidence. You are the leader. Lead with confidence. This is my biggest point on how to sing as a worship leader. As you exude confidence, others will feel comfortable in the worship setting to be led by you. If you are nervous or sound hesitant or cautious, others will feel hesitant and cautious. They will not follow you because they are nervous about where you are leading.

As the worship leader, it is important to sing in such a way that others can follow you. One of the main goals of music artists, opera singers, Broadway singers, and even local choirs is to sing in such a way that others will want to listen. As a worship leader, your goal is much different. Your goal is to sing in such a way that others will want to worship and sing along with you. You don't want them to be spectators or listeners. You want them to be active participants. So beyond singing confidently, how else can you sing to lead?

1. Begin every phrase on time and on the mic. As verse 2 is beginning, come in with the lyrics right when you are supposed to. Don't hesitate or come in too quietly.
2. Sing the correct lyrics! Lead songs you really know.
3. Sing the melody! Even though the harmony part might be really cool, you need to sing the melody because it is your voice that the congregation is following, and they need your help to know what to sing.
4. Tear down the imaginary wall between the stage and the room.
    a. Use vocal lead-in cues. I used to lead worship and give my worship team the most subtle nonverbal cues, letting them know where we were going in a song. I did it this way in the name of eliminating distractions, but I think I really did it like this because I was not confident in my leadership. Now, my favorite way to bring the room into what is happening onstage is to cue them, too! I'm leading them as well as my band. I bet they wouldn't mind having the heads-up that we are about to go back into the chorus!
    b. Once you realize you are helping to lead people somewhere, and not performing for them, you can operate in humility by putting yourself out there and doing things and saying things that are a little uncomfortable like obvious hand signals and clear verbal cues whether you sing them or say them.
    c. Make eye contact with people. Closing your eyes can be a great thing to do here and there when you lead worship. But when you do it all the time, you tend not to be in tune with the people you are leading. How can you lead the people you can't see? It's great that you are closing your eyes to eliminate distractions and better focus on Jesus, but your

role as leader also involves being aware of the room. Do they need extra help to be brought into the worship moment? Are they with you or napping?
5. Laugh or smile at your mistakes. Don't kid yourself. Most saw it. Some heard it. It can be helpful to acknowledge the big, huge mess-ups so you can get past them quicker and back into worship. The little mistakes that no one noticed don't need to be acknowledged, and you can get past them as quickly as you can and not dwell on them.

Background Vocalists (BGVs)

There are two main things to do as a BGV.

Support the Melody

Melody is important. You may have been singing for a while now when something happened. You got tired of singing melody. So, now all our singers are doubling and tripling up on harmonies so as not to sing the "boring" part. But let me tell you something: That boring part is the most important part. The room wants to sing the song with the worship team. They will hear a strong melody sung by multiple voices and jump in with the song faster and more confidently than if they heard one voice singing the melody and multiple voices singing different parts. Singing melody in unison should be done more! It is unifying, and it sounds great!

What about Harmony?

One of my close friends told me the story of when she was in kids church as an eight-year-old. She was singing during worship loud and proud from her spot in the sanctuary. At the end of one of the songs, she turned to the girl standing next to her and said, "Does it sound like I'm singing off-key? It's called *harmony*!"

I laugh when I hear this story because, for some, this statement is true. Harmony is not just singing something other than the melody. By definition, harmony notes are notes that are included in the chord of the melody. Oftentimes, harmony notes are the thirds and fifths of the melody, but not always. It just depends on the melody related to the chords being played by the instruments.

Harmony is extremely intuitive. Some people can hear a melody and innately hear the harmony part in their heads. Others will spend years training their ears to hear these harmonies, while still others will simply memorize harmony parts to certain songs. Harmony can be learned by anyone who isn't tone deaf.

The first step, if you have never sung harmony and can't pick it up on the fly, is to go back to the ear training exercise I mentioned before.

On the piano, play the 1 and then try to sing the 3. Play the 3 and see if your note matches. Play the 1 again and try to sing the 5. Play the 5 and see if your note matches.

Being able to hear the 3 and the 5 of every single note is a good start to exploring the fun world of harmony. Of course, there is more to it than that, but this will get you to a place where your ear can begin to take over and allow you to sing harmonies with less thought put into every note.

Sacrificing Personal Style for Unity

So, you want to be a Rockstar? If you haven't noticed yet, your local church worship team is not a great place for you to become a Rockstar. I used to listen to a kids' audio show called *Psalty* when I was little. In one of the episodes, a character named Charity decided she was going to be a gospel singing star. She spent most of the episode convinced that her singing voice was God's greatest gift to the world. She was arrogant, proud, and not a team player. She hurt feelings. She bulldozed team members' ideas and musical suggestions because she was the "star" and the gifted one. By the end of the episode, she had a come-to-Jesus moment and a change of heart. Charity then sang this song at the end of the episode:

Make me a servant, humble and meek. Lord, let me lift up those who are weak. And may the prayer of my heart always be, Make me a servant, make me a servant, make me a servant today.

When we approach our worship teams and our congregations, we must have this posture in our hearts. We are serving the room full of people as well as serving the rest of our team. If you are a superstar and can do all the runs and ornamentations, maybe ease up on the flashy stuff for the sake of the room. Ninety-nine percent of the room won't be able to sing with you, and you will lose room engagement.

Maybe you live in the North, but for whatever reason, you enjoy singing like a country music artist. Your worship leader doesn't sing like that, and neither does the rest of the congregation. Instead of trying to shine and highlight your awesome country twang, you could dial it back and work on blending so as not to try and stand out but serve the unified sound that the rest of the team and the room is offering up to the Lord. *The real leaders and stars are the ones who help carry the team by sacrificing personal style or even skill for the sake of unity.*

Don't get me wrong, there are times and places to have fun with vocal runs and style. Ask your worship leader or your pastor for help with this if you are struggling with proper times to let your gifting come out.

Singing from the Room

If you are a member of your church worship team, or you know you are at your core a worshipper, be a leader in the room. When I show up on a Sunday morning and I get to participate in the room during worship, I still have the mindset that I am leading the room. Leaders are never off duty. It is important we build a worship culture where our singers and musicians are worshipping offstage as well, and it is important for the room to see that. We are championing our fellow musicians and singers when we let them lead us in worship when we aren't scheduled to lead ourselves.

Rehearsals and Preparation

Practice makes permanent. And rehearsal is a practice or trial performance for later public performance. Your team rehearsal should not be the first time you are looking at the setlist for the week. You should arrive *fully* practiced and ready to play or sing your part with the rest of the team.

Oftentimes, singers show up to practice and don't even know the setlist, or they know the setlist but haven't listened to the songs or sung through them at all. What if you prepared? What if you took some time and worked on the songs? What if you practiced? I can only see good things coming from those suggestions. So, if you are ready to prepare for a rehearsal, let me give you some tips on how you could best prepare.

Make Your Own Cheat Sheet

I got this piece of advice a few years back from my favorite bass player of all time who just happens to be super-anointed and prophetic, Cassie Campbell, and it has transformed the way I learn new songs. It has massively helped me remember songs and even sing them during a service.

First, write out the words to the song you want to learn. This simple discipline helps you memorize the lyrics because, if you are anything like me, the lyrics are the last thing I learn about a song. Melody, rhythm, timing, dynamics, and even the road map are easier for me to learn than the lyrics.

A cheat sheet could have all the lyrics on it or just the starts of each section. Some of my cheat sheets are highlighted with different colors. I put the title, click speed, and the key at the top of the page. I then include the road map of the song. Let me show you an example of what I mean by road map.

Hallelujah (From our Heart to Yours)
144 BPM 6/8

Intro x2

Verse 1
Creations singing a song...

Verse 2
Perfect in all of Your ways...

Chorus
Hallelujah...

(1 measure pause)

Verse 3
Filled with wonder and awe...

Chorus
Hallelujah...

Instrumental (1x through bridge progression)

Bridge 3x
From the rising of the sun to the setting of the same
Jesus is worthy of praise
Wake up you nations and come bow your knee
Crown Him the glorious King

Chorus
Hallelujah...

Bridge 2x
From the rising of the sun...

Chorus
Hallelujah

(Crash out ending)

Example of a singer cheat sheet

♩=73 4/4   From This House   Caleb Culver
                                                 Rachel Culver

| Intro | (4 6) 5 (4 6) 5 | CH | ‖: (4 5) 6 1 5 |
| | | | (4 5) 6 1 5 :‖ |

V₁	(4 6) 5 (4 6) 5
	(4 6) 5 (1/3 4) 5	END	4 5 6 5
	(1/3 4) 5

| CH | (4 5) 6 1 5 |
| | (4 5) 6 1 5 |

| Turn | (4 6) 5 (4 6) 5 |

V₂	(4 6) 5 (4 6) 5
	(4 6) 5 (1/3 4) 5
	(1/3 4) 5

| CH | (4 5) 6 1 5 |
| | (4 5) 6 1 5 |

| Inst | 4 5 4 5 |
| | 4 5 4 5 |

| BR | ‖: 4 5 4 5 |
| | 4 5 6 5 :‖ |

| Tag | 4 5 6 5 |

Example of a Nashville Chart

It's nice to have these cheat sheets up while you lead and sing, but half the point is just the discipline of creating the cheat sheet that helps you learn the song.

Practice the Song

It's a novel idea, I know, but sing through the song a few times. Work on the trouble spots that you always graze over. Try to eliminate trouble spots. Find that harmony note you never seem to be able to find during the worship set. Sing the high parts and sing the low parts. Try singing the song in a higher key than what you will sing it in during your set. Practice singing the song in a lower key as well.

As you practice the song, here is another tip. Don't just sing through the entire song over and over again. Find the trouble spots and sing through those spots over and over again till you really get it.

Consider memorizing lyrics. Consider at least memorizing the starting lyrics of every verse. It always seems to be at the beginnings of verses that screen operators fall asleep and forget to lead you into the next part of the song. Confidence monitors are incredibly helpful, but when you really know a song, you will lead it and sing it better.

Practice with a Click Track

Is timing an issue for you? Practice singing songs and full setlists to a click track. You can get free metronome apps on your phone. Find out the click speeds for the songs you are singing and rehearse the songs while you are focusing primarily on the timing. Practice with the click till it becomes your friend and not your enemy.

Practice with an Instrument or a Track

Sometimes, we get tricked into thinking we know a song better than we really do. We sing along with an album, and it feels like we really know the song. Then we get into a set and can't remember the exact melody, or the words simply escape us. Practicing with the music but not having anyone feeding you the words and melody can be super helpful.

Singer-only Rehearsal

I have attended quite a few singer-only rehearsals over the years. These are some of my favorite rehearsals to be a part of. Often, during full band rehearsals, we can miss the nuances of style, diction, and blending. Singer-only rehearsals are a great opportunity to learn new songs, practice harmony parts, and focus on the more technical parts of singing together as a team.

During my time at IHOP–KC, I was on a worship team that would meet once or twice a month to have a singer rehearsal. Our worship leader would bring a few songs that he knew he was planning to do in the near future. We would all do some fun warmups together and then dive into the songs. We would learn the new songs together. We would assign harmony parts to different singers, practice singing the parts, and even decide when BGVs would sing and when it would be best to have just the worship leader sing. I never felt more confident going into a set than I did after one of these rehearsals. I knew what parts I was singing, and I knew when to sing. There was no guessing or trying to decipher what was needed or wanted from my leader. I felt empowered and confident.

Worship Services

There is more to leading a worship set than just singing. Preparedness, body language, facial expressions, heart posture, knowing your role, and unity are some of the other dynamics to value and consider during worship services.

Preparedness

As previously stated, walking into a worship service prepared is very important. Rehearsals, personal practice, and preparation must all be valued highly.

Body Language

You are communicating even when you are not singing. Your body communicates to the room. Do you have your arms folded, or hands on your hips, or even worse, are your hands in your pocket? These all can communicate some negative ideas like bad attitude, tiredness, or boredom. You might not feel any of those things, but your hands are saying it. Are your arms, legs, or even eyes fidgety? This can communicate nervousness or boredom.

The Hebrew words for Hallelujah (Praise the Lord) can help us with positive ways to communicate with our bodies that our heart posture is to worship and praise the Lord. These are not ideas of ways to use our body language in worship, but these are commands.

- Praise the Lord, Yahdah! Throw your hands up in praise!
- Praise the Lord, Shabach! Shout to the Lord! Celebrate!
- Praise the Lord, Barak! Kneel before Him. Bow low and worship Him!
- Praise the Lord, Zamar! Sing to the Lord! Play your instrument in praise.
- Praise the Lord, Halal! Dance and jump in His presence!

It is important to be genuine and honest in our expression of worship, but as leaders we must be aware of our body language and continually communicate our heart posture with our body.

Facial Expressions

Facial expressions could be categorized together with body language, but I chose to separate it because this subject needs its own section. Facial expressions get me into a lot of trouble. For years when I would lead worship, my heart was genuinely worshipping and connecting with God. At the same time, my face was communicating to everyone that I must have been in a lot of physical pain or deeply wounded. I looked like I just got the worst news of all time and couldn't mask the deep sorrow on my face. I started to practice smiling while singing. I began practicing allowing my face to speak to what God was doing inside me. I would feel joy on the inside during worship and let joy be on my face.

As the Lord would touch my emotions and remind me of his faithfulness, I could cry and have that look on my face, but I always aim to have my face be a representation of my true emotions in worship. For most of the time, that means my face should communicate joy, peace, love, thankfulness, etc.

Conclusion

I charge you to take your singing gift seriously. If you say all the time that you want to be a better singer, or you wish you could sing like So-And-So, then do something about it! Practice, take lessons, and learn more about your voice and what you are capable of. Become excellent at singing.

Closing Prayer

Pray this with me. It may help to read it aloud.

Father,
Thank You for the gift of singing. Thank You for the voice and the sound that You have given me. I am sorry for the times I have despised the voice and the sound that You have given me. I am sorry for being jealous of other voices. Today, I chose to thank You for my voice and say yes to growing the gift that You have given me. Would You give me grace to grow in skill? I want to be a team player on my worship team. I want to be excellent and prepare for my times of singing on the team. Help me!
*   Amen.*

Prompt 1

Identify an area of concern you have about your voice. Common concerns could be bigger and better range, better tone quality, less breathy sound, less pitchy sound, and so on.

Find a local voice teacher to help you work on these trouble spots in your voice. If this feels like too big of a step, there are hundreds and hundreds of YouTube videos with vocal teachers who give free lessons on major vocal topics. Take a YouTube lesson. Learn something new about your voice! Take a step toward excellence as a vocalist!

Prompt 2

Create a cheat sheet for one of your favorite songs to lead. It could be a breathing chart, a Nashville numbers chart, or a road map of the song.

A Testimony

I began watching worship and prayer sets from the International House of Prayer in Kansas City when I turned eighteen years old. I had just moved to Colorado to be part of a young adult internship, and I had overheard some leaders in my life sharing about their incredible (and really long) devotional times with God. I was challenged to spend more time with the Lord myself and thought listening to these worship and prayer sets would help me. The first few days were painful, to be quite honest. I kept checking the time wondering how much longer I could last.

One morning, I turned on the web stream and heard a line over and over again, "Do you know the way you move Me?" Something started shifting in me; it was almost as if, each time it repeated, it pulled back another layer, softening my heart to actually receive this truth. I had never heard a prophetic song before this one.

The song continued about weak love and how the Lord loves it and how it actually moves His heart. I hadn't really allowed myself to be weak before this point, fearful of what could happen if I wasn't the "strong one," but I had never felt weaker than in this moment. I desired relationship with the Lord but didn't know how; I wanted to trust Him, but was fearful of letting go; I wanted to believe Him, but was so hurt and broken.

"With every little glance, I'm undone. Do you know the way you move Me?"

The tears that I had refused to cry for many years suddenly came in like a flood. I was weeping, amazed that the Lord could be moved by me. Yes, the words of the prophetic singers were declaring it, but I felt the Lord's heart toward me for the first time in that moment. I'll never forget that morning and the way that specific prophetic song marked me, as the Holy Spirit softened my heart and opened my eyes to believe something I couldn't begin to grasp before.

—Kyleigh

Now is the Time

> *Sing to the Lord a new song, And His praise in the assembly of saints. Let Israel rejoice in their Maker; let the children of Zion be joyful in their King. Let them praise His name with the dance; let them sing praises to Him with the timbrel and harp. For the Lord takes pleasure in His people; He will beautify the humble with salvation. Let the saints be joyful in glory; let them sing aloud on their beds. Let the high praises of God be in their mouth, and a two-edged sword in their hand. (Psalm 149:1–6 NKJV)*

All throughout Scripture, we are commanded to sing. This command doesn't tell us to sing when we feel like it or only when opportune moments arrive. The command to sing is ongoing. Psalm 96 uses the terminology "day to day":

> *Oh sing to the Lord a new song; sing to the Lord, all the earth! Sing to the Lord, bless his name; tell of his salvation from **day to day**. Declare his glory among the nations, his*

marvelous works among all the peoples! For great is the Lord, and greatly to be praised. (vv. 1–4a ESV)

Singing isn't a hobby, skill, or gifting we should only activate on a stage. The last verse of Psalm 103:22 says, *"Praise the Lord, all his works **everywhere** in his dominion. Praise the Lord, my soul"* (NIV).

We are to do this everywhere, day to day. Sing praise to the Lord! Don't wait! The perfect time or season never comes. You never arrive at a place where it makes sense in the natural to give yourself to the calling of prophetic singing. My husband and I have counselled many young couples who want to have kids someday, but they feel like they need to wait for the perfect window of time in their lives to open up when nothing else is going on, where everything else in their life slows down or stops. We all know that season of life never comes. There is never a perfect moment to disrupt your life and have a baby. If you wait for that moment, it will never happen. Here are just a few statements I have heard regarding this idea: "I just want to get a few things in order first, then I will consider having kids," or "I just want to get my finances in order and save up X amount of dollars before having a kid." Here is the kicker: Many of the excuses for delay are legitimate and, in some cases, responsible reasons. But just like anything important and of value, you must make time for it.

> **As a prophetic singer, continue to lean into the voice of God. Don't rely on your own strength, gifting, or ability to just come through, but in humility, say *yes* to God on a new level. He wants to give you more.**

So, maybe you now recognize you are called to be a prophetic singer. I want to call you into action. At the end of every chapter, I left one or more prompts. These are mini calls to action. But as we come to the end, I want to first remind you of the practical steps you can take to grow as a prophetic singer, then commission you and give you permission to pursue this calling. So, if you are just starting out as a prophetic singer, I want to provide a few examples of how to take the next steps toward being a prophetic singer:

- Cultivate your relationship with God in the secret place.
- Worship Jesus!
- Start singing.
- Practice the skill of singing by get singing lessons or doing regular warm-ups and vocal exercises
- Read the Bible.
- Practice hearing God's voice.
- Practice singing to instrumental music, live or prerecorded.
- Practice singing around themes, scriptures, melody lines, rhythms, or chords.
- Practice making up spontaneous choruses.
- Practice with a live band.
- Attend your local church and volunteer to serve.
- Join a worship team.
- Attend and serve at local worship and prayer meetings.

In other words, do what you've been learning to do from the reading of this book and the practicing of the prompts.

If, on the other hand, you are a seasoned prophetic singer and have been doing this for years, my challenge to you is never stop being willing to grow. Continue to use the prompts provided in each chapter and switch them up a bit using different scriptures where applicable, or develop your own prompts to target areas you think need improvement. As a singer, you can get better vocally! Find a skill to practice. Maybe choruses don't come easy to you. Practice creating them. Maybe your melody lines all seem to sound the same. Notice that and practice creating new and different melodies.

As a prophetic singer, continue to lean into the voice of God. Don't rely on your own strength, gifting, or ability to just come through, but in humility, say *yes* to God on a new level. He wants to give you more. He wants to entrust you with more revelation and creative language to help express His heart to us.

I See

Before I close this chapter, I want to stir your heart with what I believe I see coming down the road. In the future, I see a generation of prophetic singers who will be used as mouthpieces of God, ones who have cultivated a life of hearing God in secret so they can make His greatness known in public as they sing.

I see a generation of worshippers, prophetic singers, and musicians who hear His voice and respond to it in the context of personal worship *and* corporate worship.

I see not the chosen few, but multitudes of singers, musicians, and worship leaders taking their place and operating in their God-given anointing and authority as prophetic leaders in the Body of Christ.

I see responsive singing only growing in the Church as the Bride of Christ learns to articulate her song to the Lord.

I see the Church singing the songs of our brothers and sisters and then also singing the song that has been deposited into us.

I see a shift in our churches from a spectator mentality to a room full of worship leaders, leading their own hearts and those around them into worship by example.

I see prophetic singers recognizing their identity before the Lord and boldly proclaiming His praises, unshaken by the turning tides.

I see *you* as one of these prophetic worshippers in this generation.

Commissioning

Arise! It is time to take your place, to wake up and say *yes* to your calling as a worshipper. You were not created to be silent, to just listen to others offer their voices in worship to the Lord. You have a sound to offer Him. It's time for you to sing! The season of singing has come! The voice of your Father in heaven is speaking to you out of Song of

> **In the future, I see a generation of prophetic singers who will be used as mouthpieces of God, ones who have cultivated a life of hearing God in secret so they can make His greatness known in public as they sing.**

Solomon 2:14, *"Let me see your face,* **let me hear your voice, for your voice is sweet***, and your face is lovely."* Another voice will not do. It must be yours. It is what He is longing for—the sound of your voice and the sound of your love.

It is time to surrender and say *yes. Creation is already singing. The rocks are ready to shout. Heaven is already declaring*—but it is your turn now! Sing the songs in your heart! You were created to do this! Sing melodies of worship to the King of kings. He has been waiting and desiring to hear the sound of *your* voice singing *your* song of praise.

I will leave you with one final prophetic song our team led us into during our True North 2020 Creative conference. The lyrics are below, but to experience the audio of this song, you can hear it in the audiobook. Receive it as your commissioning!

| **Arise! It is time to take your place, to wake up and say *yes* to your calling as a worshipper. You were not created to be silent, to just listen to others offer their voices in worship to the Lord. You have a sound to offer Him. It's time for you to sing!** |

True North 2020 Session 6 worship

Come now is the time to worship
Come now is the time to worship
Arise to your identity, ministers of the Lord!
Ones who would minister and burn before him, arise!
In our day, they will rise!
Arise, arise, arise and praise the Lord
From the North to the South to the East to the West
Arise, arise, arise and praise the Lord
Priests, ministers, prophets
Arise, arise, arise and praise the Lord
Arise, arise, arise and praise the Lord
Now is the time to Worship

Closing Prayer

Pray this last prayer with me as I pray it over you. You may want to read it aloud.

Father,

Thank You for the calling on my life to be a prophetic singer. Thank You that I get to minister to Your heart through my worship. Thank You for the honor and privilege to hear Your voice and declare it. I choose today to step into my identity.

I am done hiding and refusing to offer up my own song to You. I let go of my pride, and I choose to sing the melodies inside me. I won't withhold my love and my song.

I am done striving, trying to earn Your affection through my gifting. I want to be Your friend, like Moses. I say yes *to cultivating my life in the secret place. You are my "one thing," my desire, and my passion. Help me to always lead from this place.*

I say yes *to You. Use me however You choose. I will be one who slows down enough to listen. I will listen, and when I hear you speak, I will respond.*

Amen

Prompt

Well, here we are at the last prompt of the last chapter. You made it. I made it! It has been my great honor to walk with you through this process. If we could have spent this time in person, I would have brought you to my house, made tea or coffee, and I would have asked you about yourself, your story, and what the Lord has been speaking to you. I would have asked you to share about your times of encounter during worship and how God was moving in your life. Writing a book is so one-sided. I guess I am not surprised by that but more surprised by how much I feel the one-sidedness of it. All that to say, your voice matters, and what you have to say and who you are is valuable. I would love to learn from you one day.

Each prompt has been directly related to the contents of one chapter. For this last prompt, I would like you to reflect on the book as a whole. Reflect on what stood out to you. What did God speak to you through your times of journaling and singing your way through it? Now, make a list of 3–5 action items. Feel free to use the list of examples I gave earlier in this chapter. How will you take action? What can you put into practice today? How will you commit to grow? Remember, now is the time. It's time to sing!

About the Author

Rachel Culver is a worship leader and songwriter based out of Radiant Church in Kalamazoo, MI. Rachel and her husband, Caleb, have a long history of leading worship and raising up young singers, musicians, and worship leaders in this generation. Her heart is to see these creatives thrive in the local and global church, ushering in the presence of God, and encouraging others to do the same. Rachel has taught and coached prophetic singing at Onething Internship, Desperation Leadership Academy, and Radiant School of Worship. When she isn't singing, talking about singing, or teaching others to sing, you can find her being supermom to her two children, Aaliyah and Jordan.

CalledtoSing.com